Learning to Save the Future is an elegant book t
new world of increasing complexity and interco
italism to explore the future that depends upon   ., ... It
is a bold vision that argues for an alternative set of values beyond a techno-
economic determinism that revitalizes notions of emancipation, equality and
human freedom. Alex Means has written a compelling book with wide appeal.

Michael A. Peters, *Professor, Wilf Malcolm Institute of Educational Research, University of Waikato, New Zealand; Professor Emeritus, University of Illinois at Urbana-Champaign, USA*

Nervous about the future? You should be. Professor Means takes on the current dominant ideologies such as the faith that Silicon Valley and the creative class will rescue us from looming disasters resulting from technological and educational fixes that undermine our ability to think critically about the future. He deftly shows us how transforming education into a collaborative and just social process is central to avoiding a dystopian future and creating a world characterized by equality and democracy. A book to be read and reread for its many insights.

David Hursh, *Professor, Warner Graduate School of Education and Human Development, University of Rochester, USA*

Learning to Save the Future

Mainstream economists and Silicon Valley entrepreneurs claim that unfettered capitalism and digital technology can unlock a future of unbounded prosperity, create endless high-paying jobs, and solve the world's vast social and ecological problems. Realizing this future of abundance purportedly rests in the transformation of human potential into innovative human capital through new twenty-first-century forms of education. In this new book, Alex Means challenges this view. Stagnating economic growth and runaway inequality have emerged as the "normal" condition of advanced capitalism. Simultaneously, there has been a worldwide educational expansion and a growing surplus of college-educated workers relative to their demand in the world economy. This surplus is complicated by an emerging digital revolution driven by artificial intelligence and machine learning that generates worker-displacing innovations and immaterial forms of labor and valorization.

Learning to Save the Future argues that rather than fostering progress and mass intellectuality, educational development is being constrained by a value structure subordinated to twenty-first-century capitalism and technology. Human capabilities, from creativity to design, engineering, and communication, are conceived narrowly as human capital, valued in terms of economic productivity and growth. Similarly, global problems such as the erosion of employment and climate change are conceived as educational problems to be addressed through business solutions and the digitalization of education. This thought-provoking account provides a cognitive map of this condition, offering alternatives through critical analyses of education and political economy, technology and labor, creativity and value, and power and ecology.

Alexander J. Means is Assistant Professor in the Department of Social and Psychological Foundations of Education at SUNY Buffalo State College in Buffalo, New York.

Critical Interventions: Politics, Culture, and the Promise of Democracy
Series editors: Henry A. Giroux, Susan Searls Giroux, and Kenneth J. Saltman

Twilight of the Social: Resurgent Publics in the Age of Disposability
Henry A. Giroux (2011)

Youth in Revolt: Reclaiming a Democratic Future
Henry A. Giroux (2012)

The Failure of Corporate School Reform
Kenneth J. Saltman (2012)

Toward a New Common School Movement
Noah De Lissovoy, Alexander J. Means, and Kenneth J. Saltman (2015)

The Great Inequality
Michael D. Yates (2016)

Elsewhere in America: The Crisis of Belonging in Contemporary Culture
David Trend (2016)

Scripted Bodies: Corporate Power, Smart Technology, and the Undoing of Public Education
Kenneth J. Saltman (2016)

Gender for the Warfare State: Literature of Women in Combat
Robin Truth Goodman (2016)

Disposable Americans: Extreme Capitalism and the Case for a Guaranteed Income
Paul Buchheit (2017)

The Public in Peril: Trump and the Menace of American Authoritarianism
Henry A. Giroux (2017)

Learning to Save the Future: Rethinking Education and Work in an Era of Digital Capitalism
Alexander J. Means (2018)

Learning to Save the Future

Rethinking Education and Work in an Era of Digital Capitalism

Alexander J. Means

NEW YORK AND LONDON

First published 2018
by Routledge
711 Third Avenue, New York, NY 10017

and by Routledge
2 Park Square, Milton Park, Abingdon, Oxon OX14 4RN

Routledge is an imprint of the Taylor & Francis Group, an informa business

© 2018 Taylor & Francis

The right of Alexander J. Means to be identified as the author of this work has been asserted by him in accordance with sections 77 and 78 of the Copyright, Designs and Patents Act 1988.

All rights reserved. No part of this book may be reprinted or reproduced or utilised in any form or by any electronic, mechanical, or other means, now known or hereafter invented, including photocopying and recording, or in any information storage or retrieval system, without permission in writing from the publishers.

Trademark notice: Product or corporate names may be trademarks or registered trademarks, and are used only for identification and explanation without intent to infringe.

Library of Congress Cataloging in Publication Data
A catalog record for this title has been requested

ISBN: 978-1-138-21261-9 (hbk)
ISBN: 978-1-138-21262-6 (pbk)
ISBN: 978-1-315-45020-9 (ebk)

Typeset in Adobe Caslon Pro
by Sunrise Setting Ltd, Brixham, UK

CONTENTS

PREFACE AND ACKNOWLEDGMENTS		VIII
CHAPTER 1	SOLUTIONISM: CANCELLING THE FUTURE	1
CHAPTER 2	ECONOMISM: ETHICS AND IDEOLOGY	17
CHAPTER 3	PRECARITY: THE TICKING TIME BOMB	37
CHAPTER 4	CREATIVITY: EDUCATION AND THE COMMON	68
CHAPTER 5	DIGITIZATION: ALGORITHMIC LEARNING MACHINES	97
CHAPTER 6	AUTOMATION: DISPLACEMENT AND RUPTURE	126
CHAPTER 7	FUTURITY: CAPITALISM AND MASS INTELLECTUALITY	153
INDEX		170

PREFACE AND ACKNOWLEDGMENTS

We live in a world of increasing complexity and interconnection—a world beset by myriad problems, such as inequality, joblessness, racism and ethnic conflict, weapons proliferation, and ecological crises. It is also a world in which brilliant technologies are harnessing the power of artificial intelligence and big data to reconfigure possibilities for how we produce, work, engineer, learn, design, and engage in politics, albeit typically within a narrow set of assumptions and priorities. Within the mainstream orbit of TED Talks and Ideas Festivals, it is often assumed that capitalism and digital technology can unlock a future of endless prosperity, create endless high-paying jobs, and solve the world's vast social and ecological problems. The key to realizing this future of prosperity and abundance is often said to rest in the transformation of human potential into innovative human capital through new forms of learning. Education as a means of economic and technological innovation is the default engine of future progress.

Learning to Save the Future explores the sociological limitations of this logic. It asks the question: How can the future be said to depend on the capacity of educational systems and learning practices to produce new human capabilities such as inventiveness, problem solving, creativity, and innovative knowledge production, while at the same time the human-development mission of K-12 and higher education is eroded, defunded, and routinized, and its deeper cultural and intellectual foundations are emptied of substance? The book suggests this contradiction reflects an enclosure of sociality and politics, whereby educational imagination is constrained by a value structure subordinated to twenty-first-century capitalism and technology. Human capabilities, from creativity to design, engineering, and communication, are conceived narrowly as forms of human capital, valued in terms of economic productivity and growth. Similarly, challenges such as the erosion of livelihoods and expanding inequality are conceived as educational problems to be addressed through integrative business solutions and the digital transformation of education systems, primarily to serve corporate and financial interests, rather than the commonweal. Moreover, for perhaps the majority of people today, education is experienced as little more than an austere competition for an increasingly precarious and automated "gig" economy. The position taken in this book is that we need a different set of values for education and society beyond economic and technical determinism—values rooted in the emancipatory potential of education to enhance freedom and equality for all.

This book reflects my own idiosyncratic investigations in recent years and certainly does not exhaust the kinds of questions that could be useful for thinking about educational change. The analysis has been influenced by a desire to understand at a deeper level the economic and ideological processes that are transforming education and society including the relationship between education and the economic struggles of young people since the Great Recession, human creativity and educational administration within cognitive capitalism, and the intensifying push for "disrupting" education through Silicon Valley platforms. While attempting to foreground global processes, I draw examples mainly from the United States, which is the context where I live and work. This necessarily informs and narrows the perspectives offered. The text straddles the borders of political economy, critical theory, and sociology of education. It is not a traditional scholarly monograph, nor is it written explicitly for a general audience. It is a hybrid.

While all errors of judgment, large or small, are entirely my own, I have compiled numerous debts while writing the book. I first want to thank my partner Anna and my daughter Nina, who brought joy and laughter to my world during this project. I am also deeply grateful to my colleagues at SUNY Buffalo State not only for giving me an academic home but also for their tremendous generosity, especially Dean Wendy Paterson, Bill White, Beth Hinderliter, Reva Fish, Pixita del Prado Hill, Rudy Mattai, Laura Rao Hill, Andrea Nikisher, and Jevon Hunter. Acknowledgments also go out to Ken Saltman for his support and exchanges on various parts of this manuscript, including the suggestion of the title. Additionally, I need to thank Noah De Lissovoy, Clayton Pierce, Heather Roberts-Mahoney, Mark Garrison, Jesse Bazzul, Graham Slater, David Hursh, and Chris Arthur for their discussions on various parts of this book. Graham needs to be singled out for his willingness to suffer through early drafts of the chapters and offer his sharp and carefully considered feedback. Thank you to Henry Giroux, Susan Giroux, and Dean Birkenkamp at Routledge for their enthusiasm for the book and its inclusion in the Critical Interventions series. Finally, grateful acknowledgments for permission to significantly revise, expand, and rework the following essays: "Generational Precarity, Education, and the Crisis of Capitalism: Conventional, Neo-Keynesian, and Marxian Perspectives," *Critical Sociology*, 43, no. 3 (2017); "Creativity as an Educational Problematic in the Biopolitical Economy," in *Cognitive Capitalism, Education, and Digital Labor*, edited by Michael Peters and Ergin Bulut (New York: Peter Lang, 2011); and "Education for a Post-Work Future: Automation, Precarity, and Stagnation," *Knowledge Cultures*, 5, no. 1 (2017).

1
SOLUTIONISM: CANCELLING THE FUTURE

There is a sense today that we are witnessing a rapid evolutionary process of technological acceleration and integration. Various labels have been attached to this process, such as the *Internet of Things*, the *Internet of Everything*, or, more simply and directly, *digitization*. The most ambitious formulations suggest that in the near future all sectors of human activity and the physical environment will be integrated via sensors, data processing, algorithms, and feedback loops. Particularly relevant sectors include manufacturing (robot factories and 3D printing), finance (automated advising and trading), business logistics (Amazon drone delivery), direct exchange of services (Uber and Airbnb), urban planning (smart cities), personal health (life trackers such as Fitbit), energy (renewable "smart grids"), transportation (self-driving cars and trucks), national security (NSA's total panoptic surveillance), and education (personalized adaptive learning ecosystems). Across these diverse spheres, it is speculated that information processing and machine learning capabilities will generate new hyper-efficiencies that will enable humanity to solve some of the world's most pressing challenges, including social inequality and climate change.

Such ideas imagine the future as a computational project whereby seemingly intractable problems such as resource depletion and global poverty are rendered as technical issues to be "disrupted" through Silicon Valley business ingenuity and data platforms. The contrarian technology writer Evgeny Morozov refers to this as "solutionism," a utopian discourse that assumes all "problems are to be dealt with via apps, sensors, and feedback loops—all provided by startups."[1] To be clear, Morozov does not deny that new technology can act as a tool for the good. However, solutionism, for Morozov, is dangerous to the extent that it represents a techno-determinist vision of social change, whereby "disruptive innovation" is presented as an inevitable and inherently progressive force.[2] The result is to enclose our social imagination and replace it with what he calls "algorithmic regulation," or "Internet-centrism." The core issue is that when society is reduced to economic and technical calculations, our collective ability to define how complex problems are posed, understood, debated, and addressed is eroded.

The allure of solutionism is that it promises collective transcendence through utopian appeals to market efficiency and technical mastery beyond politics and ideology. However, as philosophers from Plato to Martin Heidegger to Donna Haraway have observed, technology is a historically determined product of human activity. It is never simply a neutral or objective mechanism. Rather, technology is always embedded within systems of meaning, value, ethics, and power that shape its development and animate its use. In the case of Silicon Valley, it has become something of a cliché and running punchline that tech companies are more interested in "saving the world" than in maximizing profit and inflating stock values. HBO's deadpan comedy series *Silicon Valley* is the model.

Although education is not a primary focus for Morozov, it is indeed central to solutionist ideology. Alongside technology, education is now widely framed as an instrument for addressing almost every conceivable global problem, from joblessness to urban redevelopment. To illustrate, in 2015, the Silicon Valley software giant Cisco Systems placed a glossy digital advertisement in the *New York Times* for its Networking Academy, a private business and technical education certificate program. Made to look like a scholarly white paper, the multi-page ad carried the title, "Launching a New Generation of Global Problem Solvers."[3] "We can use digitization along with the Internet of Everything," Cisco observes, "to help solve some of the world's most challenging problems—water scarcity, hunger, income inequality, environmental degradation, poverty, migration, and unemployment."[4] According to Cisco, the key to solving these problems is to find new approaches to education and learning so as to unleash "the power of technology to launch a generation of global problem solvers who innovate like technologists, think like entrepreneurs, and act as social change agents."[5]

Cisco's call to launch a generation of global problem solvers aligns conceptions of education, technology, and social justice with economic determinism. Stimulating economic growth and employment is here imagined as the overriding imperative of the twenty-first century. "If we can harness the power of the rocketing digitization phenomenon," Cisco states, "and align some education, curriculum, and learning to the technology job market, while driving entrepreneurship, we can use it to fuel economic growth."[6] While Cisco estimates that 280 million jobs need to be created by 2019 to close a global employment gap—which is particularly acute for young people—joblessness and lack of opportunity are here mainly conceived as education problems, the result of skill deficits and mismatches between job requirements and formal education. Cisco suggests that "a commitment to continuous learning with a strong basis in technology, entrepreneurial skills and mindset, combined with social mindedness, has become foundational to an individual's success."[7] Thus, to save the world, a generation is called upon to direct their social idealism to private investment in education to enhance their economic utility in the name of boosting GDP: in this case through Cisco's Networking Academy, where, we are told, "students not only learn the finer points of designing, building, and operating networks, they also learn about problem solving, critical thinking, collaboration, and teamwork—skills they can apply in their future education and on the job."[8] To save the world is to build human capital through education to drive productivity and innovation and therefore economic expansion. Unfortunately, most of these future problem solvers will not end up working at Cisco, as the company, like other tech giants, has been cutting employees in recent years, with 14,000 jobs lost in 2016 alone.

According to a report in *Fortune* magazine, there were a total of 63,000 job cuts across US tech firms in 2016.[9]

Cisco's call for a generation of global problem solvers raises a number of important questions. For instance, what does it mean to imagine the value and purpose of education in a world where just eight individuals now control more wealth as the bottom half of humanity, or 3.6 billion people, while the top 1 percent controls as much wealth as the bottom 99 percent globally?[10] Where the talents and creativities of millions of young people are being squandered due to inequality, poverty, racism, and social disinvestment? Where some estimates suggest half of current job categories are at risk of automation over the next two decades, potentially displacing countless workers and upending institutions? Where the erosion of democracy and generalized experiences of insecurity and alienation have given rise to a resurgent right-wing authoritarianism and proto-fascist nationalism? Where relentless attacks on science and even the truth itself enable the unhindered march of global resource depletion, species extinction, and climate disaster?

To the extent that solutionism, in both its educational and technological instantiations, presents itself as non-ideological, it is largely its economic assumptions that are left untroubled, unexamined, and unquestioned. Put simply, the *value structure* of solutionism is embedded in a denial of innovation at the level of political economy and an avowal of radical transformation at the level of technology. At the level of capitalism and politics, nothing can change. At the level of technology, everything can.[11] This reflects a paradox in popular representations of the future such as those promoted by Cisco: namely, within the boundaries of official discourse it is simply off limits to debate even minor alterations to our patterns of production, exchange, distribution, labor, consumption, and endless growth. At the same time, we are inundated with truly radical utopian visions of technological mastery and transcendence. As Matthew MacLellan observes:

> the promise of new and ever-more sophisticated technics not only drives capitalist consumerism in the West, but is readily evoked as a justification for exacerbating environmental degradation, under

the pretense that new and as-yet-unimagined technologies will miraculously emerge at some future date to remedy problems that are perceived as too difficult and too expensive to remedy in the present.[12]

Former CEO of ExxonMobil and current US Secretary of State Rex Tillerson has thus stated that climate change, if it exists, is an "engineering problem" of "adaptation" rather than an existential threat emanating from our economic systems and political decisions.[13]

Similarly, Cisco's call for a generation of global problem solvers centers education as a means of economic solutionism. It aligns the purpose of learning to economic imperatives of human capital formation, with technology positioned as a key driver. Serving the cause of economic productivity and growth is here framed not only as the core purpose of education, but also as a higher altruistic calling for young people. Through personal investments in learning and mastery of cognitive and technical skills one can not only find gainful employment or start a private enterprise, but also become a global agent of social change. Put another way, young people are enjoined to transform their creative and intellectual capacities into economically viable human capital to serve markets. This is positioned as the central means to solve the problems of the twenty-first century.

Cisco's call for a generation of global problem solvers affirms a utopian spirit attached to technological disruption and endless market expansion. Yet education today is primarily configured as a means to serve the existing order of things. Rather than offering novel visions of human flourishing and collective life, *educational value* is instead rendered in the managerial and technocratic terms of enhancing human capital to serve economic ends. Rather than the development of mass intellectuality and authentic creativity to address the foundations of global problems, *educational purpose* is oriented to decontextualized technical skills aimed at managing and adapting to their ill effects. Rather than a universal architecture oriented to directly addressing new expressions of alienation and inequality, *educational structure* functions as a mechanism of sorting and ranking in the name of meritocratic self-actualization and economic efficiency. And rather than contributing to different imaginative visions of a future in common, *educational change* is caught in a static horizon—an endless reproduction of a fractured here-and-now. Moreover, educational solutionism, as embodied by Cisco's problem solvers, represents a form of *false generosity*. It places the burden of saving the future on young people, who bear no responsibility for creating the global problems they are being tasked to solve. In short, educational solutionism cannot conceive of an *outside* to its own assumptions and structure of value, which is symptomatic of a more general inability to think beyond what Fredric Jameson refers to as the "cultural logic of late capitalism."[14]

Education scholars have long pointed to a tendency to frame social problems as educational problems.[15] Moreover, modern education has always been linked to business interests and the labor market. Horace Mann, the founder of the common-school movement in the nineteenth-century United States, located education as the means to train compliant workers, assuage class conflicts, and therein contribute to social progress. The industrial-era expansion of mass public education and administration was founded on similar principles. What is new is a sense that twenty-first-century capitalism requires distinctly new capabilities—cognitive, affective, creative, and technical—and that K-12 and higher education need to be radically remade, or "disrupted," through market mechanisms and digital technology platforms so as to unleash their potential as a force of global progress.

What needs to be understood is that the problem in educational systems and rhetoric today is not located in the focus on developing twenty-first-century human capabilities. The problem is that neoliberal models of education are rooted in reductive market values and ideologies that place restrictions on how we imagine and develop such human capabilities. Within the *rationality of neoliberalism*, or what is sometimes called *market fundamentalism*, society is remade in the image of capitalism, competition is framed as the essence of human relations, and freedom is narrowly defined as the freedom to buy and sell. Within this worldview, human capabilities, from critical thinking to social cooperation, are conceived in economic terms, inscribed as value added to productivity and growth in the economy. Intellectual and technical capability is thus understood and valued less as a public good and social process than as a prescriptive form of labor to be captured and transformed into future corporate and financial accumulation. In the language of Jan Masschelein and Maarten Simons, education is conceived as an instrumental "learning apparatus" that renders human capacities as discrete "skills" to serve economic ends such as boosting human capital, entrepreneurship, and GDP, rather than for realizing deeper forms of human freedom, solidarity, and democratic development.[16]

Importantly, however, despite the economic and technological determinism that animates the value structure of educational solutionism today, there is nonetheless a latent progressive dimension embedded within it. The anthropologist David Graeber has outlined three traditional conceptions of value that are useful to consider here:

1. "value" in the sociological sense: conceptions of what is ultimately good, proper, or desirable in human life;
2. "value" in the economic sense: the degree to which objects are desired, particularly as measured by how much others are willing to give up to get them;
3. "value" in the linguistic sense, which goes back to the structural linguistics of Ferdinand de Saussure and might be most simply glossed as "meaningful difference."[17]

Graeber argues that, by themselves, these notions of value are insufficient, largely because they do not account for ongoing processes of human action and transformation. Alternatively, Graeber develops a theory of value as "the way individuals represent to themselves the importance of their own actions."[18] "Value" in this sense is understood as a guide to individual action that is always present, but contains the potential to exceed larger social processes and systems. "Value" is thus "the way people who *could* do almost anything (including, in the right circumstances, creating entirely new sorts of social relation) assess the importance of what they do."[19] If value is the means by which we assess the importance of what we do, and also the means by which we imagine how we might do things differently, then the emphasis on transforming education into a force of global problem solving contains inherent potentiality. If value is self-representation and the immanent capacity for ethical judgment and creative human action, then we might consider how education and technology might be *revalorized* in unexpected ways to enhance mass intellectuality and our capacities to address problems that require holistic responses—economic, social, technical, educational, and political. Indeed, there already exists a rich diversity of imaginative values and practices that evade instrumental determinisms and that are actualized in the experiences of students and educators in schools and universities, and across social life, in imaginative and often unpredictable ways.

Education and technology are both crucial for developing human capabilities and confronting the dire problems we face. More than ever, we need to think expansively about educational processes and value in order to enhance and develop the forms of mass intellectuality and modes of cooperation and agency required for the future. However, as this book argues, the innovative potential of education is being constrained by the economic, social, and technological rationalities defining late capitalism. This is a book largely focused on critical theory located at the intersection of political economy and sociology of education. From a methodological standpoint, the book proceeds by way of immanent critique.[20] By immanent critique, I take inspiration from post-Hegelian critical theories that operate by demonstrating how specific social formations fail to uphold their stated aims based on their own discursive criteria and theoretical assumptions. The French sociologist Luc Boltanski describes this form of critical inquiry and analysis in terms of a normative philosophical and sociological position that details the "differential between the *official* and the *unofficial*," that is, that shows how the ideal to which an official order lays claim "does not correspond to the real conditions of its actual outcomes and, consequently, to the real condition of its members or some of them."[21] In this sense, "critique takes as its main target the fact that the order in question does not in fact conform to the values it assigns itself *in principle*."[22] While the chapters in this book each employ this general strategy, it is not a comprehensive or systematic work. My foremost concern is with education as a solutionist response to various crises associated with neoliberal society. I also point toward alternative conceptions of education and the future.

There are, of course, plenty of signs that the neoliberal order is breaking up. Challenges are now omnipresent. Official narratives that emerged in the 1990s that laid claim to an "end of history," where a Hegelian synthesis of self-regulating capitalism and democracy would ensure a boundless future of equilibrium and prosperity, have broadly collapsed. Mass economic insecurity, a culture of illiteracy and mesmerizing media spectacle, widespread confusion and disillusionment, have all contributed to a volatile political landscape and a remapping of historical coordinates.[23] Within this emerging "age of anger," as Pankaj Mishra refers to it, a resurgent right-wing populism views the future not simply as an infinite dilation of technology and capitalism at the end of history, but also as a return to a mythical glorious past.[24] Education is here typically imagined as a socializing agent in white nationalist folklore and Eurocentric assimilation.

The election of Donald Trump in the United States and the rise of the new authoritarianism more broadly reflect widespread discontent with the status quo as well as a general failure of a fragmented progressive Left to offer coherent alternatives.[25] However, it would be a mistake to read Trumpism as a break from market fundamentalism and solutionist ideology. Rather, Trumpism is neoliberalism in a more openly brutal and nationalistic form. Everything is transactional. Everything is for sale. Cruelty is celebrated. Racism and xenophobia no longer need to be hidden. Immigrants are bluntly called "rapists" and "criminals." Black Lives Matter activists are "terrorists." Journalists are "enemies of the people." All of this without the appeals to coded language defining prior conservative administrations. Likewise, billionaires rule directly without democratic pretense. ExxonMobil runs the State Department. Goldman Sachs runs the Treasury Department. And so on. The appointment of the billionaire Betsy DeVos as Secretary of Education likewise signifies an intensification of a market-driven plutocratic agenda. DeVos is an advocate of for-profit schooling through charters, vouchers, religious schools, and cyber-schools. The rhetoric of education as a means of saving the future by serving markets and thereby "Making America Great Again" remains a legitimating motif.

The temporal imagination of solutionism is thus highly conflicted. We live in a moment in which nostalgic longing for the past comingles with utopian promises of technological wonder alongside dystopian scenarios of global war, economic breakdown, radical inequality, and ecological disaster. In a jarring piece in the *New Yorker* titled "Doomsday Prepping for the Super-Rich," Evan Osnos chronicles how Silicon Valley executives and billionaires such as Peter Thiel are buying remote and securitized properties in places like New Zealand as an escape from potential civilizational collapse.[26] In essence, while Silicon Valley public relations and marketing firms spin tales of Promethean technological solutionism, tech elites are prepping for the end of the world. Taking advantage of this desire among elites for insurance against catastrophe, Osnos details how real-estate developers in the United States are tapping into a booming market in fortified luxury residences in defensible spaces such as abandoned Cold War missile silos. These underground bunker condos have their own weapons armories, sophisticated surveillance systems, and high-end amenities such as swimming pools and movie theaters. The idea here is to reproduce the gated lifestyle conditions that are fueling impending disaster in the first place. Thus, rather than investing in a future that is sustainable on a societal and ecological level, many elites are retreating into a fantasy—a privatized and militarized race to oblivion. A hedge-fund manager interviewed by Osnos, named Robert Johnson, provided a rare moment of introspection, asking: "Why do people who are so envied for being so powerful appear to be so afraid?" His response is based in recognition of extreme inequality and the systematic dismantling of the public institutions and social protections required for a humane society and functioning democracy. "If we had a more equal distribution of income, and much more money and energy going into public school systems, parks and recreation, the arts, and health care," he observes, "it could take an awful lot of sting out of society. We've largely dismantled those things."[27]

Despite visible cracks in the ideological edifice, we nonetheless seem to be stuck in a cultural condition that Mark Fisher has described as "capitalist realism," a sense of imaginative inertia and inability to think beyond neoliberal prescriptions.[28] Doomsday prepping among the super-rich is one sign of the *cynical rationality* underlying solutionism as a mode of capitalist realism. While elites buy gold-plated bunkers they are simultaneously dismantling the social foundations that might offer a more humane future for all. Meanwhile, the rest of us are told we can save the world and ourselves by pursuing more education. The sociologist Wolfgang Streeck offers a provocative observation here:

> Those who benefit from the current condition of the world are not impressed when we offer them sophisticated plans as to how they could solve our problems, because our problems are their solutions. Also, they know much more than we do, their deepest insight being that things are out of control. Their high art is to pretend that they know how to hold things together—while they work frantically to feather their nests for the moment when the system on which the rest of us depend will finally cease to function. In other words, they are playing an endgame anyway.[29]

We are living in a moment of disorientation. Alternative facts, fake news, scapegoating, narcissism, cynicism, paranoia, and conspiracy theories run rampant. The Trump administration and a fanatic right-wing congress are rolling back already tepid Wall Street regulations; instituting massive tax cuts for the obscenely rich; dismantling environmental and labor protections; trampling on indigenous land rights; instituting voter suppression aimed at minority communities; expanding the carceral and military arms of the state; and defunding and privatizing all aspects of civil society, including public schools and universities. The consequences are a continued weakening of the social fabric, despoiling of the environment, and an intensification of plutocratic rule. Whether or not Trump remains in office or is removed due to criminality or mental illness, his election will likely persist as the defining story of the next decade and perhaps beyond.

We need to begin the collective work of imagining futures beyond the one prescribed by solutionist ideology and the various crises it attempts to displace. Education, both formal and informal, is a crucial terrain in this endeavor. While formal education has limits—it alone cannot solve problems that are deeply embedded in political economy and society—schools and universities are sites where new forms of value, cooperation, technical capacity, ethical commitment, and social imagination can be nurtured and developed, thus contributing to broader projects of humanization and democratization. The Brazilian philosopher Paulo Freire is known for describing critical knowledge construction and reconstruction as "problem posing."[30] For Freire, problem posing is a humanizing approach to education that seeks to "read the world" so as to develop emancipatory forms of consciousness and action. Education, in Freire's view, is "revolutionary futurity," in the sense that history is made by human beings in the course of everyday life and is therefore never closed or finished. In this spirit, this book explores different "problem fields" associated with educational solutionism. These problem fields, elaborated below, examine contradictions and conflicts within dominant representations of education in relation to contemporary capitalism, labor, technology, and social change.

Chapter 2 of this book examines the problem of *economism* in education through an analysis of human-capital theory and its methodological and ideological dynamics and limitations. Mainstream economists, journalists, politicians, business leaders, and transnational organizations such as the World Bank and World Economic Forum routinely frame the structural problems afflicting capitalism, such as stagnation, joblessness, poverty, and inequality, as educational problems, interpreted as human-capital deficits in skills and training. Through four short theses, the chapter suggests that human-capital logics deprive education of its deeper social value and obscure power and inequality via economic assumptions detached from history and social reality. Economics has long been known as the "dismal science," and the analysis of economism in this chapter is somewhat abstract—a cognitive map of the assumptions informing the problem fields that follow.

Chapter 3 builds on this exposition of economism by foregrounding the problem of *generational precarity* to critique mainstream economic and media narratives of education as a solution to systemic instabilities. A key problem driving educational rhetoric today concerns the future economic integration of young people. It is young people who have been hit the hardest in the current era of austerity that has emerged in the aftermath of the 2008 global economic crisis. They are also the primary group targeted as a population in need of human-capital development and twenty-first-century skills to save global capitalism and promote social progress. This chapter argues that human-capital conceptions of education do not provide an adequate explanation or response to generational precarity and instead tend to normalize, individualize, and moralize the inequalities and insecurities immanent to advanced capitalism and neoliberal society.

Chapter 4 highlights the problem of *creativity* in contemporary educational organization. In recent years, there has been a growing body of work in social theory highlighting the progressive potential of creativity in relation to the knowledge economy and information revolution. For some social and educational theorists, the shift to cognitive capitalism and network technologies is generating new educational and labor arrangements characterized by creativity, openness, flexibility, and intellectuality. However, in contemporary K-12 and higher education, narrow market-driven policies are implicated in the erosion of social and intellectual foundations. This chapter argues that while the knowledge economy is often presented as a catalyst for innovation and openness that requires advanced creative, analytical, affective, cooperative, entrepreneurial, and inventive subjectivities, in practice it is embedded within reductive logics of control and forms of class and racial stratification that inhibit dynamic institutions and broad social development rooted in mass intellectuality and the common.

Chapter 5 explores the problem of *digitization* within K-12 education as a technological solution to perceived public educational failures. In light of the disappointing results of more than two decades of corporate school reforms in the United States, digital technologies are being aggressively promoted as a means of "disrupting" schooling for the economy. Modeled after digital platforms such as Netflix, Pandora, and Amazon, these technologies are being heralded as a means of "personalizing" and "customizing" education for the twenty-first century. The chapter argues that digitization can readily be interpreted as a form of instrumental rationality indicative of a control society and anti-dialogic learning apparatus that saps the creative potential of education. However, at the same time, digitization also contains strands of emancipatory possibility.

Chapter 6 addresses the problem of *automation*. While "end of work" narratives have proven unfounded, as machines have historically created many more jobs than they have destroyed, a recent wave of economists, technologists, sociologists, and journalists are speculating we may be approaching an inflection point in the automation of work. The chapter examines recent perspectives on automation that suggest the exponential advancement of technological innovation over the past four decades is creating a world in which robotics, algorithms, big data, and intelligent machines are poised to significantly alter the dynamics of education and employment. The chapter analyzes these trends in relation to the legitimacy of education as an economic discourse and argues for a new post-work vision of education.

Chapter 7 examines the problem of *futurity*. This chapter ties together the themes explored throughout the book in relation to new speculative analysis on the potential futures of capitalism through four frames—stagnation, disintegration, transcendence, and acceleration. The chapter then offers an alternative language and value system of *emancipation, democracy, and mass intellectuality* to consider different learning futures from the economic and technological rationalities defining educational solutionism.

My hope is that grappling with the paradoxes and tensions outlined in the text can be useful, even in some small way, for those interested in imagining alternative educational values and futures. We need to move beyond the reductive parameters set by neoliberal culture and its vision of society as a giant casino where the house always wins and everyone is a mark. Trumpism is an obscene caricature of this logic. We can do better.

Notes

1. Evgeny Morozov. "The Rise of Data and the Death of Politics." *The Guardian*, September 19, 2014; Evgeny Morozov. *To Save Everything, Click Here: The Folly of Technological Solutionism*. New York, NY: Public Affairs, 2014.
2. The term "disruptive innovation" was coined by Clayton M. Christensen. It refers to a new innovation that creates a new market that eventually takes over and replaces prior established businesses and systems. See www.claytonchristensen.com/key-concepts/
3. CISCO. "Launching a Generation of Global Problem Solvers." White Paper (2015). Retrieved from www.cisco.com/c/dam/en/us/solutions/collateral/industry-solutions/global-problem-solver.pdf
4. Ibid., 2.
5. Ibid.
6. Ibid., 4.
7. Ibid., 2.
8. Ibid.
9. Reuters. "Cisco's Layoffs are Just the Tip of the Spear for Tech." *Fortune*, August 18, 2016. Retrieved from http://fortune.com/2016/08/18/expect-more-tech-layoffs/
10. Oxfam International. "An Economy for the 1 Percent." Oxfam Briefing Paper, January 18, 2017.
11. See Matthew MacLellan's brilliant essay, "Capitalism's Many Futures: A Brief History of Theorizing Post-Capitalism Technologically." *Mediations* 26 (2013): 159–160. He notes: "if liberal-democratic capitalism has been endowed with a static temporality at the level of official politics, it is simultaneously narrativized, even burdened, by an almost diametrically opposed temporality at the level of technological development."
12. MacLellan, 2013, 160.
13. Chris Mooney. "Rex Tillerson's View of Climate Change: It's Just an 'Engineering Problem'." *The Washington Post*, December 14, 2016.
14. Fredric Jameson. *Postmodernism, or, the Cultural Logic of Late Capitalism*. Durham, NC: Duke University Press, 1991.
15. See David F. Labaree. "The Winning Ways of a Losing Strategy: Educationalizing Social Problems in the United States." *Educational Theory* 58, no. 4 (2008): 447–460.
16. Maarten Simons and Jan Masschelein. "The Governmentalization of Learning and the Assemblage of a Learning Apparatus." *Educational Theory* 58, no. 4 (2008): 391–415; see also Tyson Lewis. *On Study: Giorgio Agamben and Educational Potentiality*. New York, NY: Routledge, 2013.
17. David Graeber. *Toward an Anthropological Theory of Value*. New York, NY: Palgrave, 2001, 1–2.
18. Ibid., 47.
19. Ibid.
20. See Georg Wilhelm Friedrich Hegel. Translation by Arnold Miller. *Phenomenology of Spirit*. Motilal Banarsidass, 1998; Axel Honneth. *The Critique of Power: Reflective Stages in a Critical Social Theory*. MIT Press, 1993; Theodor Adorno. *Introduction to Sociology*. Stanford University Press, 2002.
21. Luc Boltanski. *On Critique*. Malden, MA: Polity, 2011, 10–11.
22. Ibid.
23. Former Greek finance minister Yanis Varoufakis outlines the story of neoliberalism's collapse: "The fetishisation of unfettered markets that Margaret Thatcher and Ronald Reagan brought to the fore in the late 1970s had been the necessary ideological cover for the unleashing of financiers to enable the capital flows essential to a new phase of

globalisation in which the United States deficits provided the aggregate demand for the world's factories (whose profits flowed back to Wall Street closing the loop nicely) ... Meanwhile, billions of people in the 'third' world were pulled out of poverty while hundreds of millions of western workers were slowly sidelined, pushed into more precarious jobs, and forced to financialise themselves either through their pension funds or their homes. And when the bottom fell out of this increasingly unstable feedback loop, neoliberalism's illusions burned down and the west's working class ended up too expensive and too indebted to be of interest to a panicking global establishment." Yanis Varoufakis. "We Need an Alternative to Trump's Nationalism. It Isn't the Status Quo." *The Guardian*, January 22, 2017.
24 Pankaj Mishra. *Age of Anger: A History of the Present*. New York, NY: Macmillan, 2017.
25 See Henry Giroux. *The Public in Peril: Trump and the Menace of American Authoritarianism*. New York, NY: Routledge, 2017.
26 Evan Osnos. "Doomsday Prepping for the Super-Rich." *New Yorker*, January 30, 2017.
27 Ibid.
28 Mark Fisher. *Capitalist Realism: Is There No Alternative?* New York, NY: Zero Books, 2009.
29 Wolfgang Streeck and Jerome Roos. "Politics in the Interregnum: A Q/A with Wolfgang Streeck." *Roar Magazine*, December 23, 2015.
30 Paulo Freire. *Pedagogy of the Oppressed*. New York, NY: Bloomsbury, 2000.

2
ECONOMISM: ETHICS AND IDEOLOGY

In 2014, the Organisation for Economic Co-operation and Development (OECD), a mainstream organization not especially known for histrionics, released a sobering forecast for the world economy titled "Policy Challenges for the Next 50 Years."[1] The report estimates that without major structural changes, global economic growth will decline over the next five decades to 2.7 percent, with a recessionary rate of 0.54 percent in OECD nations and 1.86 percent in non-OECD nations. Additionally, by 2060, the report estimates that global inequality will increase by 30 percent as new technology threatens to displace large numbers of low- and mid-skilled jobs and demographic shifts and mass migration place new burdens on state budgets, heightening the likelihood of social conflict and political destabilization. Furthermore, unless carbon emissions are dramatically reduced, the OECD projects that climate change—which is viewed here as an economic problem to be addressed with market-driven policies—could curb GDP by another 1 percent globally and 6 percent across Asia in the same time frame. Such outcomes would almost certainly exceed the suffering imposed by the Great Depression, only this time inflected by mounting ecological crises.[2]

The "Policy Challenges" report succinctly describes a deep and ongoing structural crisis of capitalism. The stark realities described by the OECD and future projections of stagnation, inequality, and instability also reflect a crisis of mainstream economic thought as well as social and educational imagination. Of the many recommendations made in the OECD report to renew growth and stave off various crises over the coming decades, investments in human-capital education arguably take center stage, with repeated emphasis on the "importance of knowledge-based capital for growth," commitments to "education and skills" with a "focus on early years," "life-long learning initiatives," and "funding reforms to ensure sufficient growth in tertiary education."[3] This reflects a widely held belief that human-capital education contains almost magical economic properties. What is unique about the "Policy Challenges" report, however, distinguishing it from similar documents, is that it locates educational reform and human-capital development in the context of projected long-term global economic decline.

Prior to 2008, economic stagnation was not an issue taken seriously by mainstream economists and/or the institutions that employ them. In the early 2000s, those such as Ben Bernanke, former chairman of the US Federal Reserve, suggested that at some point in the 1990s the United States and other wealthy nations had entered a halcyon period known as the Great Moderation, where the "objective laws" of modern economics and monetary policy had been firmly established, much like the General Theory in physics.[4] Apart from the occasional recessions that emerge from the normal fluctuation of the business cycle, self-regulating markets, human-capital upgrades, and innovation would ensure equilibrium, distributed prosperity, and growth in perpetuity.

Much has occurred since 2008, when out of the ashes of the Great Moderation rose the Great Recession, from which the world economy has yet to fully recover. The "Policy Challenges" report concisely describes an ongoing set of crises—economic stagnation, deepening inequality and precarity for workers and the poor, and ecological fragility. Wolfgang Streeck has suggested that these crises have become so pervasive that they are leading to the "rediscovery of the older notion of a capitalist society—of capitalism as a social order and way of life, vitally dependent on the uninterrupted progress of private capital accumulation."[5] A small number of mainstream economists such as Lawrence Summers, Tyler Cowen, and Robert Gordon have also begun to openly debate, alongside their heterodox interlocutors like Streeck, the possibility of long-term, "secular" stagnation in the global economy.[6] Despite the profound challenges facing global capitalism, commitments to mainstream economic orthodoxy remain firmly entrenched. This is perhaps nowhere more evident than in assertions that education combined with new technology can serve as a panacea for resolving twenty-first-century economic problems.

Human Capital as a Neoliberal Avatar: Four Theses

The idea that formal education can resolve economic problems reflects the post-Keynesian tilt of the economics discipline that germinated in the post-World War II era and came to prominence after the economic crises of Fordism and "stagflation" in the 1970s, particularly under Ronald Reagan in the United States and Margaret Thatcher in the United Kingdom.[7] The now dominant "orthodox" or "mainstream" perspective can be understood as emerging from the cross-of two schools of economic thought: first, the Austrian School and its emphasis on the superior efficiency and information-processing capacity of markets versus state administration, particularly the work of Carl Menger, Ludwig von Mises, and Friedrich von Hayek, the latter of whom published the anti-planning manifesto *The Road to Serfdom* in 1944; second, the Chicago School, associated with Milton Friedman, Gary Becker, Eugene Fama, Robert Lucas Jr., and others at the University of Chicago who have developed various neoclassical postulates concerning rational choice, human-capital theory, and the general equilibrium tendencies of markets.

While neoclassical perspectives are dominant in mainstream economics, both the Austrian and Chicago Schools have contributed to the development of neoliberal ideology. I define neoliberalism here as a sociopolitical rationality and historical phase of capitalism that strategically works to transform all aspects of state policy and social life to reflect and serve the demands of markets and elite corporate and financial interests. Importantly, mainstream economics and neoliberalism are not monolithic. They are neither internally consistent nor without contradiction. They are also often applied in highly variable ways and are path dependent institutionally and geographically. Nonetheless, they reflect general patterns of thought and action germane to understanding broad historical tendencies and social formations. Such general patterns associated with mainstream economics and neoliberalism can be understood as constituting an ideological field of market fundamentalism, which is the dominant belief, now bordering on religious devotion, that if left unburdened by state interference and the "irrational" demands of democratic polities for protections and alternatives, self-regulating markets will inherently maximize the conditions for economic growth and thus the common good.[8]

Within this view, education is singularly imagined as a vehicle for raising the productivity of labor as a basis for economic growth and innovation. Such ideas are based on a view of human beings as embodied economic capacities, or human capital. Economists associated with the Chicago School, such as Jacob Mincer, Gary Becker, and Theodore Schultz, developed the theory of human capital in the 1950s and 1960s as a way of interpreting a correlation between the post–World War II economic boom and educational expansion.[9] They speculated that education enhanced the marginal productivity of labor and therefore contributed to growth, employment, and rising wages. As Gary Becker succinctly puts it, "since human capital is embodied in knowledge and skills, and economic development depends on advances in technological and scientific knowledge, development presumably depends on the accumulation of human capital."[10]

Since the 1960s, human capital has been studied across the spheres of human health, education, child rearing, and crime policy through the neoclassical approaches of Becker, Milton Friedman, Robert Lucas, and James Heckman, as well as through the "new growth theories" associated with Robert Solow and Paul Romer.[11] Romer's work on the role of human capital, technology, and innovation as "endogenous" factors to economic growth has been particularly influential in education and transnational policy circles since the 1990s. Based on these ideas, it is argued that globalization and information technologies have elevated high-skilled, analytical, technical, and creative forms of human labor as central to economic growth. This has placed a premium on educational systems as sites of knowledge production and job training. Eric Hanushek and Ludger Wößmann capture these ideas in a World Bank report titled "The Role of Education Quality for Economic Growth":

> Education can increase the human capital in the labor force, which increases labor productivity and thus leads to a higher equilibrium level of output. It can also increase the innovative capacity of the economy—knowledge of new technologies, products, and processes promotes growth. And it can facilitate the diffusion and transmission of knowledge needed to understand and process new information and to implement new technologies devised by others, again promoting growth.[12]

Hanushek and Wößmann here articulate the view of human-capital education (HCE) as a means to increase the productivity of human labor, and therefore technological innovation and economic growth. These characteristics of HCE reflect a historical transition in economic governance from a prior era of liberalism and Keynesian state-managed capitalism to reliance on neoliberal logics as the basis for state policy and educational organization. This has reoriented not only the *structure of education systems* to reflect market rationalities and corporate imperatives in a time when governments have abandoned prior forms of social investment, but also the *broader narratives* that shape how societies and individuals have come to conceive the *purpose and value* of education primarily as a human-capital vehicle. As Fazal Rizvi and Bob Lingard succinctly observe:

> With the rejection of the ideas associated with the Keynesian welfare state, governments have increasingly preached a minimalist role for the state in education, with greater reliance on market mechanisms. As educational systems around the world have become larger and more complex, governments have been either unable or unwilling to pay for educational expansion, and have therefore looked to market solutions. This has led to an almost

universal shift from social democratic to neoliberal orientations in thinking about educational purposes and governance, resulting in policies of corporatization, privatization and commercialization on the one hand, and demand for greater accountability on the other ... educational purposes have been redefined in terms of a narrower set of concerns about human capital development, and the role education must play to meet the needs of the global economy and to ensure competitiveness of the national economy.[13]

Stephen J. Ball further notes the transformation of educational value and purpose:

Education is now regarded primarily from an economic point of view. That is, the role of education as a producer of labour and skills and of values, like enterprise and entrepreneurship, and of commercial "knowledge," as a response to international competition. The social and economic purposes of education have been collapsed into a single, overriding emphasis on policy making for economic competitiveness and an increasing sidelining (other than in rhetoric) of the social purposes of education ... This is evident across a whole variety of policy texts in virtually every nation on the planet.[14]

There is now a wide scholarly literature on human-capital theory as well as neoliberal education and its diverse manifestations.[15] This book does not wish to rehash these issues in systematic detail. In what follows, this chapter offers four short theses that highlight conceptual, ethical, and political problems associated with human-capital theory as the dominant neoliberal paradigm orienting educational organization today. My focus here is not on either proving or disproving the relative contribution to growth and employment offered by human-capital investments in education. Historical evidence on this question is complex and contradictory, and the following chapter will address such issues from a particular vantage point: that of the economic insecurities afflicting young people. Here I am interested in how the assumptions underlying

HCE obscure and fail to index key underlying dynamics that shape the educational and social fields. Thus, rather than systematic or totalizing critique of economic conceptions of education, I offer a brief synthesis of key methodological, ethical, epistemological, and structural problems relevant to the chapters that follow.

Thesis 1: Method

HCE is based on ahistorical methodological assumptions that assume social good is ensured by insulating markets from the social itself. The central operating principles of HCE can be traced to the classical liberal tradition, and specifically to Adam Smith's *Wealth of Nations*. In this book, Smith suggests that through the supposedly "natural" pursuit of their own self-interest to "truck, barter, and exchange," individuals generate collective prosperity and wellbeing.[16] As Smith put it, "it is not from the benevolence of the butcher, the brewer, or the baker, that we expect our dinner, but from regard to their own self interest."[17] The key for Smith is, of course, the "invisible hand," or the sphere of market exchanges, through which competitive self-interest and private economic decisions are supposedly transformed into an objective force of social progress.

With this formulation, Smith provided a foundation for modern economics, whereby economic laws are derived from metaphysical premises regarding human nature and society. Extending from Smith, contemporary economic science can be understood as an ideological reading of capitalist society as a non-ideological field. The notion that efficient markets are analytically distinct from ethics and politics is a core feature of neoclassical economics, including human-capital theory. For instance, in his essay "Methodology of Positive Economics," Milton Friedman, mentor to Gary Becker, John Lucas Jr., Robert Fogel, and others at the University of Chicago, where human-capital theory originated, argued that economics can and should be rendered as an "objective science," concerned only with "what is" and not "what ought to be." It is understood as being "in principle independent of any particular ethical position or normative judgments."[18]

HCE is likewise presented as an objective scientific discourse that is independent of subjective judgments and ideology. Relying heavily on mathematical modeling and prediction regarding educational contributions to productivity, HCE is presented simply as a neutral mechanism for nations and individuals to maximize their own competitive advantage and, in doing so, to ensure prosperity and meritocratic outcomes. However, as far as it is embedded within neoclassical economic doctrine, HCE is guilty of what Joseph Schumpeter referred to as "methodological individualism," the idea that social realities and structures can be reduced to the self-interested actions and egoistic motivations of individuals.[19] This myopic view of social reality contributes to what the French economist and critic of mainstream economics, Thomas Piketty, describes as "a childish passion for mathematics and for purely theoretical and often highly ideological speculation at the expense of historical research and collaboration with the other social sciences."[20] This disconnection from history and social science serves to obscure the simplistic ideological assumptions regarding human nature and social order that guide mainstream economics through a thin veneer of scientific objectivity and mathematical complexity. As James Galbraith notes, "a complaint about the argument can be deflected, most easily, on the ground that the complainer must not understand the math."[21]

As formative critics of market fundamentalism such as Karl Polanyi have long documented through anthropological research on diverse patterns of human organization, there is no historical basis underlying the assumption that human nature coheres to the rational agent constructed by market liberalism and neoclassical economics. Rather, degrees of individualism, greed, altruism, and cooperation are primarily determined by prevailing historical and social conventions.[22] As Polanyi outlined in his magisterial book *The Great Transformation*, "the alleged propensity of men to truck, barter, and exchange is almost entirely apocryphal … the outstanding discovery of recent historical and anthropological research is that man's economy, as a rule, is submerged in his social relationships."[23] Moreover, markets are never "natural" in either their creation or operation, nor do they obey the predetermined "objective" laws posited by economic science. To borrow another concept from Polanyi popular in economic sociology, markets are always "embedded" within a web of social relations and are thus always enabled and constrained by human decision and action.[24] However, as Polanyi argued, a distinct feature of market fundamentalism is to assert that markets are autonomous from the social and ethical realms. This assertion that the market is a separate "natural" sphere effectively shields economics from politics and subordinates life to economic calculation.

HCE similarly functions to subordinate education to economic rationalities. However, educational purpose and organization are always embedded within social relations and subject to ethical and political judgments. As Tal Gilead has argued in his analysis of human-capital logic, "educational policy based solely on economic advice is bound to be educationally impoverished" as "orthodox economic theory deliberately excludes aspects that are extremely important to educational policy, such as human improvement, human agency, and normative considerations."[25] While human-capital theorists such as Gary Becker do acknowledge that individuals may act according to a variety of motivations other than simply economic ones, HCE is nonetheless presented as an objective science free from subjective values and politics that can ensure efficiency and maximize social good. This tends to treat educational policy and institutions as black boxes removed from questions of ideology, power, authority, values, and human action.

Thesis 2: Capital

HCE reifies labor as capital "stocks" and education as enterprise. As opposed to a human and/or citizen with natural rights such as in the classical liberal tradition, or even a worker alienated from the fruits of their labor in the Marxian tradition, human-capital theory renders human beings foremost as *produced flows* of capital. Classical political economy accorded human labor a special role as the primary generative source of value. In his *Second Treatise of Government*, John Locke characterized productive labor as the means by which private property (and therefore also for Locke European colonialism and imperialism) is legitimated and transformed into a natural right. In the Ricardian and Marxian traditions, it is likewise human labor that is the source of capitalist profit, understood as the difference between wages allocated and the excess value produced by labor in the production process. As articulated in the work of Jacob Mincer, Gary Becker, and Theodore Shultz and others associated with the Chicago School of economics in the 1950s and 1960s, neoclassical theories dramatically reconfigure labor as human capital. Rather than simply a commodity and exogenous input, human capital views human labor as a differentiated, endogenous factor of production and exchange—i.e. a distinct form of *capital,* or "stock" of intangible human attributes and capacities garnered specifically from investments in education, training, skill building, and lifelong learning.

This formulation has a number of consequences. Foremost, HCE dissolves labor as a "concrete" or "abstract" power in the Marxian lexicon into a bundle of *technical capacities* (hard skills applicable to tasks) and *differentiated embodiments* (soft skills such as grit, tenacity, teamwork, resilience, sociability).[26] This reduces the full expression of human attributes, creativity, cooperation, and agency to a technical economic calculus, or decontextualized set of "skills." Such a reduction is troubling not only from a standpoint of full human development in all its richness and complexity, but also for the development of creative and scientific capacities that require capacious human cooperation and imagination. This represents not only the "disenchantment of politics by economics," as William Davies, riffing on Max Weber, has described neoliberalism, but also *the disenchantment of the human by capital.*[27] Additionally, as human-capital "stocks" are said to accumulate through the totality of experience, HCE draws all aspects of social life, particularly schools and families, into the calculation of human-capital investment.[28] All of society is conceived as a "factory"—or, in terms suitable to the digital age, as a "network"—for human-capital production in the service of capital writ large.

While human-capital theorists such as Eric Hanushek have focused on improving educational "quality" by making it more "efficient" and "accountable" through market reforms and corporate management strategies, HCE tends to recognize only *a singular form of capital* (namely "skills") derived from a relatively simplistic input (investment)/output (skilled workers) binary model of education.[29] It therefore ignores what the sociologist Pierre Bourdieu identified as the multidimensional forms of *financial, cultural, and social capital* embedded in class, race, and gendered power structures that intimately shape the educational and social fields. As Bourdieu states, "from the very beginning, a definition of human capital, despite its humanistic connotations, does not move beyond economism and ignores, *inter alia*, the fact that the scholastic yield from educational action depends on the cultural capital previously invested by the family."[30] On a micro level, human capital does not register how differential cultural advantages and disadvantages transmitted in families and tracked to class, gender, and race inequities shape the dynamics of power and outcomes within institutions such as schools, either in the official curriculum (transmission of socially sanctioned knowledge) or the hidden curriculum (symbolic interactions, rituals, and practices).[31] On a macro level, human capital likewise does not index the relative "correspondence" between structural class, race, and gender inequalities and stratified educational organization and outcomes, and/or how positional conflicts over livelihoods and educational credentials have intensified in the present context of global competition, precarious employment, wage stagnation, and austerity.[32] Moreover, HCE presents a false equivalency between individual ownership of human capital and owners of private capital (wealth, investments, assets, productive enterprise), thereby obscuring the structural power asymmetries central to capitalism as a system.[33]

Similar to the Parsonian functionalist sociologies that peaked in the 1950s and 1960s, HCE assumes a relatively smooth, meritocratic, and conflict-free chain of educational production, whereby educational investments and the rational self-interest of individuals increase the supply and productivity of human capital that supposedly always realizes its true value according to the productive value it adds to the economy, which in standard doctrine is said to be determined by efficient price signaling through the self-regulating mechanisms of supply and demand. Ultimately, with the disappearance of class, labor, race, and gender, HCE imagines education as a meritocratic enterprise for remaking persons and their productive capacities into capital "stocks" to be traded for jobs and money. This ignores how status relations, positional conflicts, and asymmetries of power shape educational conditions and outcomes, particularly in a moment of expanding economic and social inequality. Moreover, HCE closes off a more capacious understanding of human labor and consciousness, not simply as a reflection of static economic logics and models, but as inherently creative and generative forces immanent to social life. From the unpaid care work predominantly performed by women to a vast array of socially valuable work performed in communities by all, human capital has only one measure of value, which is value added to the private accumulation of capital.

Thesis 3: Governance

HCE is more than simply an economic or educational discourse, but reflects the neoliberal reorganization of society. While the conversation thus far points to the methodological and conceptual orientation of HCE, it has told us relatively little about its content as a distinctive political rationality. Within human-capital theory, every worker becomes a capitalist and every human being a CEO of his or her own entrepreneurial self, reimagined as a distinct firm or speculative life project.[34] In Kantian terms, humans become imagined and learn to imagine themselves, their labor, and their education strictly as *a means* of economic performativity and investment, rather than as *ends in themselves*. Drawing on Michel Foucault's concept of governmentality, Michael Peters has referred to this as "new prudentialism" and Maarten Simons, similarly, as "learning as investment."[35] New prudentialism and learning as investment are conceptual tools to describe the *constructivist orientations* of neoliberal rationality and the key role of formal education within the recalibration of the state and the making of neoliberal subjects.

Recent scholarship by Angus Burgin, Jamie Peck, Philip Mirowski has provided fascinating insights into the historical reassertion of free-market orthodoxy and the development of neoliberalism. They have tracked how the movement originally began to germinate and coalesce far outside of the ideological mainstream with initial meetings of the Mont Pelerin Society in the 1940s. These invitation-only meetings of fellow travelers were led by Hayek and were organized around shared concerns over the "threat to civilization" posed by all forms of state planning. With the eventual revolt of the business class and corporate elites in the 1970s and 1980s against the apparent "excess of democracy," as Samuel Huntington famously referred to it, that accrued to workers under Keynesian labor compacts and throughout the society, and that was expressed by labor, civil rights, feminist, and anti-war movements of the 1960s, a highly coordinated effort emerged to reassert control and bring the ideas of thinkers such as Hayek and Friedman into the mainstream. This included the creation of endowed chairs and tenure lines in university economics departments and the development of new media and activist think tanks such as the Heritage Foundation and the American Enterprise Institute.

Whereas classical liberalism and mainstream economists celebrate decentralization and assert the necessity of shielding markets from state interference, a chief characteristic of neoliberal policy has been the bold *remaking of the state* at the national and transnational levels. As a number of analysts such as David Harvey, Jamie Peck, and Wolfgang Streeck have detailed, in contrast to the dominant Keynesian rationalities orienting economic administration in the post-World War II era, neoliberal rationalities are not aimed at regulating capitalism and/or promoting growth through balancing returns to labor in relation to capital, but rather seek to *aggressively rework and remobilize the state* to empower private capital and expand markets into all aspects of social life, from endlessly using public money to bail out financial institutions, to militarizing social control (as evidenced by ballooning prison populations), to enacting educational policy where human-capital theory is explicitly called upon to promote market-based strategies of privatization, standardization, and integration of corporate managerialism.[36] What might be described as "neoliberal nationalism" signaled by Trumpism in the US and right-wing populism in Europe and beyond can be imagined as an intensification of market fundamentalism combined with racial resentment and xenophobia acting as ideological cover for state-sanctioned kleptocracy.[37] Rather than a populist revolt against the excesses of neoliberalism, the new authoritarianism represents an evolving mutation of it.

The recalibration of the state is simultaneously mirrored in the way neoliberal logics function to transform our sense of self, relationships, values, and actions. The neoliberal subject is not simply an individual endowed with natural rights and/or a rational chooser bent on maximizing their own liberty and self-interest as stipulated in the classical liberal tradition, but is charged with viewing their own subjectivity and their own conditions of existence strictly through the optic of economic risk management and entrepreneurial calculation within a society redefined around competition, narcissism, and celebrity worship.[38] New prudentialism and learning as investment require that we all must learn to view ourselves as a field of marketable entrepreneurial potentials to be endlessly cultivated. Philip Mirowski captures this logic beautifully:

> The fragmentation of the neoliberal self begins when the agent is brought face to face with the realization that she is not just an employee or student, but also simultaneously a product to be sold, a walking advertisement, a manager of her resume, a biographer of her rationales, and an entrepreneur of her possibilities. She has to somehow manage to be simultaneously a subject, object, and spectator. She is perforce not learning about who she really is, but rather, provisionally buying the person she must soon become. She is all at once the business, the raw material, the product, the clientele, and the customer of her own life.[39]

As HCE is viewed as the source of a human being's value, rendered as value added to economic productivity, then inequalities simply reflect either failing public educational systems and/or the failure of individuals to prudently invest in their own education and skill upgrading in order to take advantage of the meritocratic opportunities provided by the market. Within this new *ethic of the self*, HCE emerges as perhaps the central justification for the distribution of life outcomes, as individuals assume ever more responsibility for their own economic security and wellbeing through the shrewd development of their personal "stock" of human capital via formal education and training. This has an intensive *moral dimension* as those in the labor market that fail to upgrade their human capital via educational investments and individual risk management are viewed as solely responsible for their own life condition, thereby absolving the state, elites, and the economic system, while *legitimating neoliberal life and death by the market*.[40] This is something like what the great Polish political economist Michal Kalecki was referring to when he once observed that "the fundamentals of capitalist ethics require that 'You shall earn your bread in sweat'—unless you happen to have private means."[41]

Thesis 4: Power

HCE obscures fundamental exclusions and functions to enclose countervailing forms of knowing, being, and acting in world. Neoliberalism serves to flatten meaningful difference and obscure inequalities through an abstract conception of universality conceived in terms of atomized notions of rational utility maximization and market competition. Within this frame, class, race, gender, physical, and sexual differences are collapsed into a unitary, all-encompassing vision of economic man, or *homo economicus*.

This image of the human being as embodied human capital screens out the fullness and richness of human experience, difference, value, cooperation, and capacities outside economic calculations. It also narrows our understanding of sociality and the common good, framing both as expressions of self-interest and impersonal market signals and fluctuations. An effect is to capture and enclose the educational and social imagination.

When human capital originated in the 1950s and 1960s, a common criticism at the time was that, not unlike slavery, the theory imagined human beings in terms of their economic functions, as machinery or as commodities like any other to be bought and sold. As Francis Ewald notes in a discussion with Gary Becker and Bernard Harcourt in 2012:

> From an economic perspective, the vision of man becomes very, very poor. Man is a being who responds to stimuli from the environment, and we can modify his behavior with a choice of stimuli ... In this respect, the result of the theory, perhaps, is to produce a vision of man that is very impoverished. We start with the theory of the agent and we can understand how people make decisions in

certain contexts, with certain information, and so on. But at the end, we have a poor behaviorism.[42]

Such sentiments can also be found within the traditions of classical liberalism. J.S. Mill, for instance, offered a rebuke to conceptions of human beings as capital, stating that "the human being himself ... I do not classify as wealth. He is the purpose for which wealth exists."[43] However, insofar as human capital presents a unitary vision of human being within the terms of market calculation and rational action, it tends to replay the *Eurocentric and patriarchal* embodiments and the enduring legacy of *colonial epistemologies and ontologies* inherent in constructions of the modern liberal humanist subject.[44] For its part, human capital inscribes an image of the human within an enclosed set of registers reflecting market essentialism—the neoliberal self is known and can be manipulated, quantified, and optimized as a consuming subject that learns to negotiate risk and reward within a field of market action. This is a human being conceived as a set of static economic drives as opposed to a set of open potentials. This is a unified and monolithic human outside sociality as opposed to a human defined by difference as a universal commonality embedded in history and reflective of distinct social relationships.

Moreover, as Wendy Brown has noted, the subject of human capital is defined less by guaranteed civil rights and social protections (however unequally they have been ascribed historically within liberalism) than simply by the injunction to compete in the market to maximize and leverage their portfolio value of human-capital "stocks" through formal education and lifelong learning. As a result, "when the political rationality of neoliberalism is fully realized, when market principles are extended to every sphere, inequality becomes legitimate, even normative, in every sphere."[45] In this sense, the market rationality embodied within HCE separates conceptions of human being, knowing, and acting from the historical and political dynamics responsible for ongoing modes of inequality, insecurity, racism, exclusion, and alienation.[46] For Brown, the stakes are not simply in the legitimation and normalization of injustice and inequality, but the effacement of democracy. Neoliberal rationality's drive to reconfigure "all aspects of existence in economic terms," she argues, "is quietly undoing basic elements of democracy. These elements include vocabularies, principles of justice, political cultures, habits of citizenship, practice of rule, and above all, democratic imaginaries."[47]

The erasure of countervailing forms of solidarity and imagination is not simply a by-product of neoliberalism, but is in fact immanent to it as an ideology and political project. Within human-capital logics there is simply no *time horizon* other than the one provided by endless accumulation of competitive human (labor) and financial (profit) capitals. Similarly, the value and purpose of education are imagined as reflecting and serving these market priorities, no matter how illogical or destructive they turn out to be. We need alternative values and forms of imagination oriented to futures for education and society beyond the logics of human capital and market fundamentalism. HCE conceals institutional realities and attempts to redefine human action and consciousness as a reflection of ahistorical economic doctrine. Similarly, HCE can only conceive of education as derived from and working to serve markets and GDP, as opposed to as authentic processes of human development, mass intellectuality, and social change. This curtails the ability of educational systems and societies to raise basic questions concerning dominant social arrangements and to conceive of alternatives. HCE infringes upon finding creative solutions beyond the boundaries of official discourse to the *deep crisis of political economy* signified, for instance, by the OECD's predictions of long-term secular stagnation and deepening global inequality over the coming decades. We thus need a different set of registers and values for K-12 and higher education that reconnects human capabilities to the values and conditions in which human freedom, reciprocity, pluralism, solidarity, equality, and mass intellectuality can thrive. Ultimately, we need new models of political economy and education rooted in a vision of *futurity*—an openness to alternative possibilities for living and being: an *after* to economism.

Notes

1. OECD. "Policy Challenges for the Next 50 Years." *OECD Economic Policy Papers*, no. 9, July 2014. Retrieved from www.oecd.org/economy/Policy-challenges-for-the-next-fifty-years.pdf
2. The OECD report projects that by 2060, biodiversity is expected to greatly decline, 40 percent of the world's population will live in areas of high water scarcity, deaths linked to air pollution will double, and "disruptive climate change is likely to be locked in as a result of a large increase in greenhouse gas emissions." Ibid., 30.
3. Ibid., 6–7.
4. Ben Bernanke. "The Great Moderation." In Evan F. Koenig, Robert Leeson, and George A. Kahn (Eds.), *The Taylor Rule and the Transformation of Monetary Policy*. Stanford, CA: Hoover Institution Press, 2004.
5. Wolfgang Streeck. *How Will Capitalism End? Essays on a Failing System*. New York, NY: Verso, 2017, 47.
6. Tyler Cowen. *The Great Stagnation: How America Ate all the Low-Hanging Fruit of Modern History, Got Sick, and Will (Eventually) Feel Better*. A Penguin eSpecial from Dutton. Penguin, 2011; Robert J. Gordon. *The Rise and Fall of American Growth: The US Standard of Living since the Civil War*. Princeton University Press, 2016; Lawrence H. Summers. "US Economic Prospects: Secular Stagnation, Hysteresis, and the Zero Lower Bound." *Business Economics* 49, no. 2 (2014): 65–73.
7. For a detailed history charting the triumph of free-market orthodoxy in the late twentieth century see Angus Burgin. *The Great Persuasion: Reinventing Free Markets since the Depression*. Cambridge, MA: Harvard University Press, 2012; see also, Philip Mirowski. *Never Let a Serious Crisis Go to Waste: How Neoliberalism Survived the Financial Meltdown*. New York, NY: Verso Books, 2013.
8. See David Harvey. *A Brief History of Neoliberalism*. Oxford, UK: Oxford University Press, 2005; Jamie Peck. *Constructions of Neoliberal Reason*. Oxford, UK: Oxford University Press, 2010.
9. Joel Spring. *Economization of Education: Human Capital, Global Corporations, Skills-Based Schooling*. New York, NY: Routledge, 2015.
10. Gary Becker quoted in ibid., 19.
11. Alan Burton Jones and J.-C. Spender. *The Oxford Handbook of Human Capital*. Oxford University Press, 2011.
12. Eric A. Hanushek and Ludger Wößmann. "The Role of Education Quality for Economic Growth." *World Bank Policy Research Working Paper* 4122 (2007).
13. Fazal Rizvi and Bob Lingard. *Globalizing Education Policy*. New York, NY: Routledge, 2009, 2–3.
14. Stephen J. Ball. (Ed.). *Educational Policy: Major Themes in Education*. Volume 1. New York, NY: Routledge, 2017, 8.
15. For one of the most incisive overviews of human-capital theory see Emrullah Tan. "Human Capital Theory: A Holistic Criticism." *Review of Educational Research* 84, no. 3 (2014): 411–445. On neoliberal education, see Stephen J. Ball. *Global Education Inc: New Policy Networks and the Neo-Liberal Imaginary*. New York, NY: Routledge, 2012; Mark Olssen, John A. Codd, and Anne-Marie O'Neill. *Education Policy: Globalization, Citizenship and Democracy*. London, UK: Sage, 2004. David Hursh. *The End of Public Schools*. New York, NY: Routledge, 2016. Kenneth J. Saltman. *Capitalizing on Disaster*. New York, NY: Paradigm, 2007; Graham Slater. "Education as Recovery: Neoliberalism, School Reform, and the Politics of Crisis." *Journal of Education Policy* 30, no. 1 (2015): 1–20; Noah De Lissovoy. *Education and Emancipation in the Neoliberal Era:*

Being, Teaching, and Power. New York, NY: Palgrave, 2015; Noah De Lissovoy, Kenneth J. Saltman, and Alexander Means. *Toward a New Common School Movement*. New York, NY: Paradigm, 2014. Alexander J. Means. *Schooling in the Age of Austerity: Urban Education and the Struggle for Democratic Life*. New York, NY: Palgrave Macmillan, 2013.
16 Adam Smith. *The Wealth of Nations (Books 1–3)*. New York, NY: Penguin Classics, 1999, 117.
17 Ibid., 119.
18 Milton Friedman. "The Methodology of Positive Economics." In *Essays in Positive Economics*. Chicago, IL: University of Chicago Press, 1953, 3–43.
19 Joseph Schumpeter. "On the Concept of Social Value." *Quarterly Journal of Economics* 23 (1909): 213–232.
20 Thomas Piketty. *Capital in the Twenty-First Century*. Cambridge, MA: Harvard University Press, 2014, 32.
21 James Galbraith. *The End of Normal*. New York, NY: Simon & Schuster, 2014, 67.
22 Karl Polanyi. *The Great Transformation: The Political and Economic Origins of Our Time*. Beacon Press, 1944. See also Chris Harmen. *A People's History of the World: From the Stone Age to the New Millennium*. New York, NY: Verso, 2008. David Graeber. *Debt: The First 5,000 Years*. Brooklyn, NY: Melville House, 2014.
23 Polanyi, 1944, 48.
24 Fred L. Block. *Postindustrial Possibilities: A Critique of Economic Discourse*. Berkeley and Los Angeles: University of California Press, 1990; Greta R. Krippner. "The Elusive Market: Embeddedness and the Paradigm of Economic Sociology." *Theory and Society* 30, no. 6 (2002): 775–810.
25 Tal Gilead. "Educational Policymaking and the Methodology of Positive Economics: A Theoretical Critique." *Educational Theory* 64, no. 4 (2014): 365.
26 Samuel Bowles and Herbert Gintis. "The Problem with Human Capital Theory: A Marxian Critique." *American Economic Review* 65, no. 2 (1975): 74–82.
27 William Davies. *The Limits of Neoliberalism: Authority, Sovereignty and the Logic of Competition*. Sage, 2016.
28 James J. Heckman. "Policies to Foster Human Capital." *Research in Economics* 54, no. 1 (2000): 3–56. Some economists like Heckman refer to those aspects of human-capital capabilities derived explicitly from the total aggregation of one's life experience and relationships as social capital. But this is to reduce what we mean by the social to economics, which in my view is deeply problematic from the standpoint of both full human development and the functioning of a robust and critical democracy.
29 Eric A. Hanushek and Dennis D. Kimko. "Schooling, Labor-Force Quality, and the Growth of Nations." *American Economic Review* 90 (2000): 1184–1208.
30 Pierre Bourdieu. "The Forms of Capital." In Imre Szeman and Tim Kapsoy (Eds.), *Cultural Theory: An Anthology*. Wiley-Blackwell, 2011, 83.
31 See Michael Apple, *Education and Power*. Routledge, 2013.
32 On "correspondence theory" see Samuel Bowles and Herbert Gintis. *Schooling in Capitalist America*. New York, NY: Basic Books, 1976. For analysis of intensifying competition and positional conflict for credentials see Phillip Brown, Hugh Lauder, and David Ashton. *The Global Auction: The Broken Promises of Education, Jobs, and Incomes*. Oxford University Press, 2010.
33 Bowles and Gintis, 1976.
34 See Wendy Brown. *Undoing the Demos: Neoliberalism's Stealth Revolution*, Brooklyn, NY: Zone Books, 2015.
35 Michael A. Peters. "The New Prudentialism in Education: Actuarial Rationality and the Entrepreneurial Self." *Educational Theory* 55, no. 2 (2005): 123–137; Maarten

Simons. "Learning as Investment: Notes on Governmentality and Biopolitics." *Educational Philosophy and Theory* 38, no. 4 (2006): 523–540.
36 See Harvey, 2005; Peck, 2010; Streeck, 2017.
37 Sasha Breger Bush. "Trump and Neoliberal Nationalism." *Common Dreams*, December 24, 2016. Retrieved from www.commondreams.org/views/2016/12/24/trump-and-national-neoliberalism
38 Drawing on Michel Foucault's lectures, there are now many studies that have made this observation concerning neoliberal subjects. See Wendy Brown, *Undoing the Demos* for a synthesis of these ideas.
39 Mirowski, 2013, 108.
40 Wendy Brown, 2015.
41 Michal Kalecki. "Political Aspects of Full Employment." *Political Quarterly* 14, no. 4 (1943): 322–330. This essay is best known for theorizing the economic links between fascism and capitalism. Kalecki argues that fascism is a mode of governance in which capitalists are willing to accept Keynesian-style state intervention to support full employment and high profitability on the condition that the state also maintain the hierarchical structure of capitalism based on worker discipline and political control. While unregulated capitalism can be harmful to profitability and employment due to a tendency toward the overaccumulation of capital, such crises can also lend support for fascism among both workers and capitalists as a way of stimulating profitability and full employment, albeit at the expense of freedom, rights, and democracy.
42 Gary S. Becker, François Ewald, and Bernard E. Harcourt. "Becker on Ewald on Foucault on Becker: American Neoliberalism and Michel Foucault's 1979 'Birth of Biopolitics' Lectures." *Coase-Sandor Institute for Law & Economics Working Paper* no. 614, 2012. My friend and colleague Mark Garrison is in the process of writing a brilliant analysis of the links between neoliberalism and behaviorism.
43 J.S. Mill quoted in Tan, 2014, 412. On human capital and slavery also see Clayton Pierce. *Education in the Age of Biocapitalism*. New York, NY: Palgrave, 2012.
44 See De Lissovoy, 2015.
45 Wendy Brown, 2015, 64.
46 De Lissovoy, 2015.
47 Wendy Brown, 2015, 17.

3
PRECARITY: THE TICKING TIME BOMB

Scholars and journalists now often use the term "precarity" to describe experiences of insecurity and austerity in the contemporary period.[1] Precarity typically refers to an economic and existential condition accompanying the shift to unstable, temporary, and insecure employment. This is usually contrasted to a prior era of stable employment and middle-class prosperity associated with the New Deal consensus that was initiated by Franklin D. Roosevelt in the aftermath of the Great Depression and which paved the way for the so-called Keynesian "golden age" of labor and social compacts in the post-World War II era. Precarity is thus used to describe *post-welfare social arrangements* and the economic decline of the middle and working class within affluent Western nations such as the United States, as these are really the only historical contexts in which a broad swath of workers has been able to win progressive income and benefit guarantees—although racism and sexism meant the benefits were unevenly experienced and distributed. This social order, which continues to dominate prevailing social expectations of economic progress and stability, only held for a brief time prior to the crises of industrial Fordism in the 1970s and the subsequent transition to globalization and neoliberalization in the 1980s and 1990s. Thinkers such as Brett Neilson and Neil Rossiter have thus argued that precarity is really a return to "normal" patterns of inequality and insecurity associated with the historical geographies of capitalism, rather than an exception.[2] For instance, precarity is viewed as a return to the inequality of the late nineteenth-century Gilded Age.

Generational Precarity

In recent years, particularly since the global economic crisis that began in 2008, young people have experienced the most severe consequences of declining economic security. New terms such as "generation jobless," "the new underclass," "generation screwed," and "the precariat" have entered the popular lexicon to describe a generation of young people confronting potentially destabilizing levels of inequality, debt, unemployment, and underemployment. It is often suggested in the media and in the business press that the solution to "generational precarity" is more and better education. It is argued that educational systems need to be more closely aligned with emerging human-capital imperatives in order to produce the high-skilled, flexible, and entrepreneurial workers required to stimulate innovation and invent the jobs of the future. However, transformations in the global division of labor, such as the reality of vast global labor surpluses, combined with new disruptive technologies associated with "platform capitalism" and the flexible "gig" economy, have contributed to generating new uncertainties regarding the future economic prospects of young people across societies.[3]

Although gains have been made since the depths of the Great Recession, the future economic integration of the young remains a daunting global challenge. According to a 2015 baseline report prepared by a World Bank consortium, young people between the ages of 15 and 29 years now constitute 40 percent of the world's unemployed and are up to four times more likely than adults to be unemployed and underemployed.[4] Nearly one third of the world's young people can be described as NEETS—not in education, employment, or training. Of the additional one billion young people expected to enter the global labor market by 2026, only 40 percent are expected to acquire jobs that currently exist, presumably due to the reorganization of labor markets in relation to new technology and machine-learning capabilities. In a stunning revelation, the report estimates that the global economy will have to create 600 million jobs over the next ten years, or more than five million a month, just to maintain current levels of youth employment. "The world's youth are unable to find sustainable and productive work," notes Mathew Hobson, a lead author of the report; this "contributes to inequality, spurs social tension, and poses a risk to present and future national and global prosperity and security."[5]

Generational precarity is often referred to as a "ticking time bomb" in the media. Writing in *Bloomberg Business*, Robert Coy observes that "the fissure between young and old is deepening," with the emergence of "a lost generation of the disaffected, unemployed, or underemployed— including growing numbers of recent college graduates for whom the post-crash economy has little to offer."[6] Adding statistical weight to these remarks, a 2016 investigative report by *The Guardian* titled "Revealed: The 30-Year Economic Betrayal Dragging Down Generation Y's Income" details that in every category, from poverty, to income, to job security, to debt, to home ownership, to savings, young people today are facing declining economic fortunes and circumstances.[7] "Prosperity has plummeted for young adults in the rich world," the report notes; "millennials have suffered real terms losses in wages in the USA, Italy, France, Spain, Germany and Canada."[8] This is "likely to be the first time in industrialized history, save for periods of war or natural disaster, that the incomes of young adults have fallen so far when compared with the rest of society."[9] Using household survey data, the *Guardian* study analyzed the incomes and wages of young people in 8 of the 15 largest developed economies, which together account for 43 percent of global GDP. The data reveal that young people have lower relative incomes than prior generations and have a more difficult time achieving economic security and independence. For instance, it is becoming almost impossible for young people in many countries, such as the United Kingdom and Australia, to buy homes: housing prices have skyrocketed, particularly in cities. Young people in the United States find it increasingly difficult to afford higher education without taking on crippling levels of student debt. As of 2016, total US student loan debt amounted to $1.3 trillion, and one in four former students were in default.[10] Unable to find adequate employment and affordable housing, many young people are stuck living at home with their parents—nearly one in four recent US graduates were in this situation in 2016.

Statistics like these are not abstractions. Employment insecurity and declining real wages, soaring costs of college tuition, and staggering levels of student debt mean that vast numbers of young people are facing a future of great uncertainty and hardship. The negative impacts are felt in elevated rates of poverty among youth, significantly reduced lifetime earnings and savings, and profound anxiety, stress, depression, and self-blame. For instance, research shows that millennials experience much higher rates of anxiety and stress about the future than prior generations and that they also commit suicide at higher rates as well. A report by the *Chronicle of Higher Education* reveals that 25 percent of US college students have a diagnosable mental illness and that suicide is currently the second leading killer of college students, a rate that has more than tripled since 1950.[11]

While they are often derided as coddled and lazy, as a cohort, millennials tend to work longer hours than baby boomers did—typically for low pay, and often for free, as unpaid internships have become a norm.[12] It is crucial to understand, of course, that generational precarity is unevenly experienced and reflects class, race, and gender differences and expanding inequalities across societies.[13] I personally see these patterns with the working-class students I teach at the State University of New York in Buffalo, who often work multiple low-wage jobs—sometimes 40 hours a week or more—while also attending school full time, which at my campus is 15 credit hours, or five classes. Students often express frustration with the way things are, but have difficulty imagining things could change, or that they could be the agents of change. As Jennifer Silva has documented in her monograph *Coming Up Short*, this generation of working-class young men and women are coming of age in a vastly different economic and socio-psychological landscape defined by "low expectations of work, wariness toward romantic commitment, widespread distrust of social institutions, profound isolation from others, and an overriding focus on their emotions and psychic health."[14] As Silva documents, neoliberal culture has taught young people that the key to success is to rely only on oneself and to get a college degree, narratives they have dutifully internalized. For many, however, the prospect of achieving economic independence and security appears harder and harder to attain, particularly as college is no longer any guarantee of a secure job.

It should be noted that young people from working-class, immigrant, and racially marginalized backgrounds face many additional barriers to acquiring secure economic pathways and livelihoods. They are more likely to face discrimination in hiring and to have to cope with geographical and social isolation that limits access to affordable transportation, housing, well-resourced schools, and employment opportunities. Additionally, the United States has the highest rate of child poverty of all affluent societies, with nearly one in four young people under 18 currently living below the poverty line ($24,250 for a family of four). The country also maintains profound inequalities in public educational investment and has deepening levels of racial and class inequality and segregation across society. For example, between 2000 and 2014 the number of public schools in the United States with 90 percent low-income and 90 percent racial-minority students more than doubled.[15] As decades of social science make clear, inequality, poverty, racism, and segregation produce negative health and social conditions that directly erode the human development capacity of schools and create stratified educational outcomes.[16] Moreover, inequality and racial segregation can be directly tracked in employment. For instance, according to the Center for American Progress, African American youth make up only 16 percent of Americans aged 20–24, but they constitute 23 percent of young adults inactive in the labor market. Similarly, Latino youth make up 21 percent of Americans aged 20–24, but constitute 23 percent of labor-inactive young adults.[17] These figures do not include the disproportionate number of young people of color who have been discarded by the new economy and warehoused in expanding prison systems through the war on drugs and what the sociologist Loic Wacquant evocatively calls the "criminalization of poverty."[18]

Framing the Crisis: Overeducation and Undereducation

Media representations often frame generational precarity as an educational problem. For instance, in Canada, where I lived for several years during the height of the Great Recession, the generational crisis is often said to derive from *overeducation* (or at least education of the wrong type—too many humanities degrees, for instance). Young people in Canada, it is argued, are facing a job market oversaturated with college and university graduates, which means that there are simply more credentialed job seekers than there are jobs that require advanced levels of education and credentials. Anxieties reflecting the overeducation narrative are widely discussed in the Canadian media. For instance, *Maclean's* magazine ran a story describing this generation of Canadian post-secondary college and university graduates as "history's most cultivated underclass."[19] A CBC documentary titled "Generation Jobless" covered similar ground. It posed the question: "Why are so many young Canadians overeducated and unemployed?"

> There was a time when a University degree assured you of a good job, good pay and a comfortable life. Not anymore. Today, the unemployment rate for young people in this country is close to 15%—double that of the general population. But the real crisis is the increasing number of university and college grads who are underemployed – scraping by on low-paid, part-time jobs that don't require a degree.[20]

Despite roughly similar post-secondary attainments (Canada is ranked second in the OECD and the US fifth), the popular narrative is quite different in the United States. While represented as an educational problem, generational precarity is said to stem from *undereducation*.[21] From this perspective, the US educational system is said to be failing to provide enough skilled graduates relative to demand, and this is thought to hamper economic growth and job creation even though university attainment has risen to historic levels in the United States. Unlike in Canada, the educational system in the United States is said to be in terminal crisis. This point of view is represented in countless news stories and editorials such as Thomas Friedman's books and opinion pieces in the *New York Times*. It is succinctly articulated by a report by Anthony Carnevale and Stephen Rose titled "The Undereducated

American," in which Carnevale and Rose argue that the United States needs 20 million additional college graduates by 2025 to keep up with rising demand for highly educated workers in the economy.[22]

What is important to note here is that narratives that understand generational precarity through the lens of undereducation and overeducation tend to obscure more than they reveal. After all, how can too much education and too little education both be responsible for the problem? This is not to suggest that undereducation (as an absence of formal skills) does not render many young people unqualified for certain jobs, or that overeducation (as a surplus of formal skills, or of the wrong kind of skills) does not render many young people overqualified for certain kinds of jobs. These two factors are coextensive and variable upon a host of complex geographical, demographic, economic, social, technological, educational, and political factors. However, as the eminent sociologist David Livingstone has detailed, "the dominant historical tendency—with the notable exception of the early post-World War II years—has been for the supply of educationally qualified job seekers to exceed the demand for any given type of job."[23] Adhering to this empirical insight, in the following sections I detail that neither undereducation nor overeducation provide an adequate explanation for the precarious conditions confronting young people today, largely due to flawed mainstream neoliberal assumptions regarding the relationship between education, employment, and capitalism.

Precarity as a Human-Capital Problem

Media narratives such as the undereducated American and overeducated Canadian are based in mainstream economic perspectives that suggest technological change and the level of human-capital development are the central factors determining relative levels of employment and inequality. For instance, University of Chicago economist Raghuram Rajan argued in his influential book on the 2008 financial crisis, *Fault Lines*, that challenges to growth and employment in the United States can be located in the gap between the supposed demand for high-skilled workers and their supply. "Perhaps the most important factor is that although in the United States technological progress requires the labor force to have ever-higher skill levels," Rajan observes, "the educational system has been unable to provide enough of the labor force with the necessary education."[24]

Rajan frames this argument in terms of "skill-biased technological change" (SBTC), which stipulates that a rising supply of skilled labor generates employment as it keeps pace with new technological requirements. This is a revised version of Say's Law, named after the nineteenth-century economist Jean Baptiste Say, which stipulates that a rising supply (in this case of skilled labor or human capital) always creates its own demand. Workers with high skill levels drive innovation and growth, it is argued, which then increases demand in employment. In turn, workers assume ever more responsibility for acquiring increasingly advanced levels of education and skills training necessary to keep up with changes in technology.

A recent influential articulation of these ideas can be found in the work of Claudia Goldwin and Lawrence Katz, who have analyzed the relationship between education, technology, and employment through the perspective of SBTC.[25] They argue that the most significant factor in determining levels of employment as well as income distribution is the capacity of educational systems to meet the human-capital requirements of new technology. They argue that economic expansion and reductions in inequality in the United States and other industrialized economies during the middle part of the twentieth century, which they refer to as the "Human Capital Century," were driven by mass expansion of public education that kept pace with technical innovations that then generated an attendant demand for enhanced skills. They state:

> We have emphasized the existence of an ongoing and relentless race between technology and education. Economic growth and inequality are the outcomes of the contest. As technological change races forward, demands for skills—some new and some old—are altered. If the workplace can rapidly make adjustment, then economic growth is enhanced without greatly exacerbating inequality of economic outcomes. If, on the other hand, the skills that are

currently demanded are produced slowly and if the workforce is less flexible in its skill set, then growth is slowed and inequality widens. Those who can make the adjustments as well as those who gain the new skills are rewarded. Others are left behind.[26]

The SBTC thesis coincides with a now widespread claim that the decline of economic opportunity and mobility among the young is the result of a skills/jobs mismatch, where young workers are said to lack the right skills for current job requirements. Goldin and Katz, as well as others committed to the SBTC and skills/jobs mismatch explanations, argue that increasing the number of college graduates and refocusing their training will generate employment and reduce inequality as an increasing supply of skilled workers emerges to meet and stimulate new demand. MIT economist David Autor and his colleagues have offered a complementary perspective to the SBTC and skills/jobs mismatch theses.[27] They observe that new labor-saving technology and enhanced mobility of capital and production under globalization have "polarized" Western labor markets. This has "hollowed out" middle-income employment, which includes many "routine" jobs that are easy to automate and/or outsource, such as in manufacturing. Simultaneously, they claim that the bulk of job growth has occurred at the top of the wage hierarchy in analytically demanding sectors such as STEM and finance, and at the bottom in low-wage service jobs that are difficult, if not impossible, to automate or outsource. Autor and Dorn observe:

> Computerization is not reducing the quantity of jobs, but rather degrading the quality of jobs for a significant subset of workers. Demand for highly educated workers who excel in abstract tasks is robust, but the middle of the labor market, where the routine task-intensive jobs lie, is sagging. Workers without college education therefore concentrate in manual task-intensive jobs—like food services, cleaning and security—which are numerous but offer low wages, precarious job security and few prospects for upward mobility.[28]

Autor and Dorn are not overly pessimistic about the future of work and their prescriptions for young people are closely aligned with the SBTC and skills/jobs mismatch arguments. "Citizens should invest more in their education," they argue. "Spurred by growing demand for workers performing abstract job tasks, the payoff for college and professional degrees has soared; despite its formidable price tag, higher education has perhaps never been a better investment."[29] In sum, the SBTC, skills/jobs mismatch, and polarization theses suggest that the answer to resolving generational precarity is to reform education so as to elevate and tailor the skills of the young to meet and stimulate demand in employment.

Precarity and the New Feudalism

In his book *Average Is Over*, George Mason University economist Tyler Cowen extends these arguments while offering a decidedly more pessimistic assessment of the challenges facing the next generation. "The labor market troubles of the young," he writes, "are a harbinger of the new world of work to come."[30] Cowen suggests that in the future, young people with the right education, skills, and training will continue to gain a competitive advantage and garner a "wage premium" over their less educated peers. However, he describes an emerging zero-sum world in which intelligent machines will increasingly substitute for human labor and in the process radically remake the employment structure. "Whether we wish to call those machines 'AI,' 'software,' 'smart phones,' 'superior hardware and storage,' 'better integrated systems,' or any of the above. This is the wave that will either lift you or that will dump you."[31] He writes:

> The key questions will be: Are you good at working with intelligent machines or not? Are your skills a complement to the skills of a computer, or is the computer doing better without you? ... If you and your skills are a complement to the computer, your wage and labor market prospects are likely to be cheery. If your skills do not complement the computer, you may want to address that mismatch. Ever more people are starting to fall on one side of the divide or the other. That's why *average is over*.[32]

The idea that "average is over" signals Cowen's belief that current economic and technological trends mean extreme bifurcation of employment and income is inevitable and unalterable. In his view, advances in robotics, automation, and computing power are creating a "hypermeritocracy" in which the highly educated and motivated few (top 1–15 percent) will perform demanding cognitive work and lead enriching lives, while the majority will face growing economic redundancy and diminished opportunity. One of the few growth industries that Cowen identifies for young people who may not be technically inclined is in the provision of new personal services to the rich. He states:

> We can expect a lot of growth in personal services, even if those jobs do not rely very directly on computing power. The more the high earners pull in, the more people will compete to serve them, sometimes for high wages and sometimes for low wages. This will mean maids, chauffeurs, and gardeners for the high earners, but a lot of service jobs won't fall under the service category as traditionally construed ... It sounds a little silly but making the high earners feel better in just about every aspect of their lives will be a major source of job growth in the future.[33]

Cowen's description of the future is dystopian. However, it is also typical of mainstream economics in that it positions self-regulating markets as the only viable means of organizing society and distributing ethical social outcomes. There is no alternative but to adapt by reconfiguring our educational systems to prepare the young physically and psychologically for a future of Darwinian competition over increasingly scarce jobs and opportunities. Young people are to entrepreneurially invest in their human capital through education and lifelong learning in order to add value to the high-tech economy or suffer the consequences. Without too much hyperbole, the logical extension of his argument would be that for K-12 and higher educational systems to provide pathways for young people into the future, highly automated job market, they should downsize in all areas—such as literature, philosophy, political science, fine arts—that are unrelated to the core "value-adding" STEM fields, while also creating new degree programs in areas designed to serve the rich, such as elite spa therapy, plastic surgery rehabilitation, and butler etiquette. Ultimately, Cowen imagines a future mirroring a digitized, neo-feudal version of Downton Abbey. "At some point it is hard to sell more physical stuff to high earners," Cowen observes, "yet there is usually a bit more room to make them feel better. Better about the world. Better about themselves. Better about what they have achieved."[34]

Cowen's vision, of course, reflects a right-wing cultural politics that justifies the degradation of existential possibilities for young people through the conflation of personal virtue and market justice. Cowen argues that a majority of young workers in the United States and elsewhere are simply not hirable due to character flaws, such as "laziness" in young men and what he refers to as "strong baby lust" in young women. These young people, he says, either refuse to upgrade or are incapable of upgrading their human capital. While crude, such views are hardly unique. For instance, in his book on the white working class, *Coming Apart*, the conservative social scientist Charles Murray argues that the problems confronting young people cannot be understood separately from the apparent disintegration of self-restraint, personal discipline, and "family values" among the middle and working classes. Similarly, *New York Times* columnist David Brooks suggests that the rich simply have better values, work harder, are inherently moral and deserving, and instill the right attitude for educational achievement and social striving in their children.[35]

Within mainstream economics and conservative rhetoric, the mitigation of precarity is thus positioned as a task for education and human-capital cultivation—but this will only succeed, it is argued, if the middle and working classes embrace a new ascetic moralism and inculcate a renewed sense of grit and stoic discipline in the young.[36] For his part, Cowen, unlike other mainstream economists, observes that there will likely be increasingly large numbers of superfluous workers in the future, primarily as the result of accelerating automation. However, as he cannot imagine any alternative to unfettered capitalism, he suggests that sprawling shantytowns be built on the outskirts of major cities to provide cheap living conditions for those that fail to maximize their human capital through the proper exercise of moral rectitude and competitive individualism.[37]

It is in neoliberal narratives like Cowen's that the human-capital framing of generational precarity as an educational problem reveals itself for what it is: a blatant form of ideology that justifies an economic system based upon the enrichment of the few and the exploitation of the many. Here, technology becomes an alibi for a host of broader contradictions, tensions, and conflicts immanent to the political and moral economy of global capitalism and US society. Education, in turn, is not only positioned as a means for producing skills, dispositions, and capacities to meet the demands of employers, but also as an ethical scene of *subjectification* whereby young people are to develop a gritty *resilient self* that submits to the rhythm of supposedly immutable economic laws and a new disciplinary regime of technologically mediated and precarious work.

Precarity as a Policy Problem

In his *General Theory of Employment, Interest, and Money*, John Maynard Keynes offered a systematic critique of the assumptions underlying such orthodoxy.[38] Like Marx had in a previous era, Keynes offered a devastating rebuke to Say's Law by arguing that self-regulating markets are not naturally inclined toward either equilibrium or full employment. For Keynes, employment is not set by the supply or price of labor, but rather by total consumption and spending as related to aggregate demand in the economy. As total amount of production tends to exceed consumption in any given period of time, Keynes argued that the state must step in to provide policies and investments that support full employment and help shore up demand. According to Keynes, orthodox economic theories of self-regulating markets were thus based on stark ideological mystifications.[39]

Writing in *The Guardian*, Dean Baker of the Center for Economic and Policy Research echoes Keynes by observing that mainstream economic explanations such as those offered by Goldin and Katz, Autor, and Cowen regarding the primacy of education and technology serve to obscure the core issues driving generational precarity. He states:

> This story is comforting to elites because it means that inequality is something that happened, not something they did. They won out because they had the skills and intelligence to succeed in a

dynamic economy, whereas the huge mass of workers that are falling behind did not. In this story the best we can do for the left behinds is empathy and education. We can increase their opportunities to upgrade their skills in the hope that more of them may be able to join the winners.[40]

Such observations are not meant to deny the powerful role of education and technology in shaping labor-market conditions. For instance, a recent study by Carl Benedikt Frey and Michael Osborne of the University of Oxford has suggested that up to 47 percent of job categories in the United States are at high risk of automation over the next two decades.[41] Other analysts, such as Stuart Elliot, have put this figure as high as 80 percent. Chapter 6 will return to the question of automation and its potential impact on educational futures and the future of livelihoods. For now, what is essential to point out is that the dislocating effects of new technology for the economic prospects of young people have little relation to the relative educational and/or skill levels of the population.

Like Baker, a number of liberal economists, such as Joseph Stiglitz, Jeff Madrick, Robert Reich, and Paul Krugman, argue that mainstream narratives of SBTC and skills/jobs mismatch do not provide adequate explanations. Drawing broadly on Keynesian principles, they reject supply-side rationalities that suggest human-capital development generates its own demand and thus that education is the primary cause of and/or solution to generational precarity. In contrast, they observe that in the current economic climate, affluent societies such as the United States have simply not been creating enough jobs relative to demand. They also note that the fastest growing job opportunities are in low-wage sectors that do not require advanced educational credentials, skills, or training. For instance, the National Employment Law Project has found that employment losses in the United States during the Great Recession were concentrated in middle- and upper-income employment, while employment gains during the "recovery" have been heavily concentrated in low-wage sectors such as home health, aids, fast-food work, and security—lower-wage jobs constituted 22 percent of recession losses but 44 percent of recovery growth; middle-wage jobs constituted 37 percent of recession losses but only 26 percent of recovery growth; higher-wage jobs constituted 41 percent of recession losses and only 30 percent of recovery growth.[42] Additionally, a 2016 study by economists from Harvard and Princeton found that 94 percent of the ten million jobs created between 2005 and 2015 were in temporary, contract, or part-time "gig" jobs across a number of different, typically low-wage fields.[43] Moreover, and contrary to Autor's "jobs polarization" thesis, there simply has not been any growth in high-wage employment over the last decade. Jeff Madrick describes the consequences for young people of a labor market of expanding low-wage service jobs:

> Between 1992 and 2000, 18 million people joined the workforce. Between 2000 and 2010, only 2.2 million were able to join. With far fewer jobs available, those with more experience get picked first, while those entering the workforce for the first time get picked last. The recession has exacerbated this trend, as older workers delay retirement in hopes of rebuilding the savings lost in the downturn. Those aged fifty-five and older are the only group whose labor-force participation has actually increased in recent decades. They are taking the part-time jobs kids used to get as store clerks and cashiers ... Meanwhile, recent college graduates are left to take the jobs that once went to high school graduates and even dropouts.[44]

Across wealthy OECD economies like the United States, college graduation rates have risen to historic highs at the same time that job prospects and wages for college-educated workers have fallen. For instance, according to the Economic Policy Institute, "between 2000 and 2012, the real (inflation-adjusted) wages of young high school graduates declined 12.7%, and the real wages of young college graduates declined 8.5%."[45] This reflects, of course, that many college and university graduates are stuck in jobs that do not require advanced skills, training, or even a degree. Furthermore, the Center for American Progress has reported that "the share of Americans ages 22 to 27 with at least a bachelor's degree in jobs that don't require that level of education was 44% in 2012," while another "year-long survey ending in July 2012 of 500,000

Americans ages 19 to 29 showed that 63% of those fully employed had a bachelor's degree, and their most common jobs were merchandise displayers, clothing-store and cellular phone sales representatives."[46] Furthermore, former US Treasury Secretary Lawrence Summers has observed a steady decline in workforce participation rates and job availability within the United States despite historic rates of educational expansion:

> Job availability is already a chronic problem ... Consider what has happened to 25- to 54-year-old men, a group that is instructive to consider because there is a strong prevailing expectation of universal work. Some 50 years ago, 1 in 20 men between those ages was out of work. Since that time the workforce has gotten substantially healthier and better educated. Indeed, the improvements in education have been far greater than anything we can expect to take place over the next two generations. Yet it is a reasonable estimate that 1 in 6 men between 25 and 54 will not be working if and when the economy returns to normal cyclical conditions.[47]

While those with advanced levels of education do maintain a competitive advantage in the labor market and the elevation of skill levels does play a role in economic development, aggregate demand for middle- and high-income employment is eroding. The majority of jobs being created are clustered in precarious, low-skilled service niches that do not require high levels of education or technical ability. In the STEM fields, which are presented as a cure for almost every conceivable economic malady, evidence suggests that the US educational system is producing more graduates each year than there are jobs available in those fields, raising further empirical questions concerning the SBTC and skills/jobs mismatch arguments. Widely respected think tank and policy organization the Economic Policy Institute reports that for every two students graduating with a STEM degree from a university each year, only one is hired directly into a STEM job.[48] In information science and engineering, the United States graduates 50 percent more students than are hired into those fields each year, while real wages for these workers have plateaued at late-1990 levels.[49] Among computer-science graduates who do not end up entering the IT field, 32 percent say it is because IT jobs are simply unavailable.[50] This partially reflects how US technology companies have used temporary foreign workers on H-1B visas as a means to drive down the wages of domestic cognitive workers.[51]

All this is not to argue that there are not areas in which business and industry are having a hard time filling positions, but rather to say that the reasons, as those such as Peter Cappelli of the Wharton School at the University of Pennsylvania have documented, typically do not reflect an overall skills shortage or mismatch in the US labor market.[52] Rather, in an effort to download costs to public educational systems, corporations have cut or eliminated on-the-job training that they used to provide, and are often offering such low pay that they cannot find skilled workers willing to take open positions. Where there are shortages of skilled workers in the United States, such as in the skilled trades, it often reflects policy decisions in secondary and higher education since the 1990s, where vocational education was devalued and eroded under the rationale that everyone was going to become a knowledge worker or entrepreneur—a rationale that has not panned out.

Moreover, substantial evidence indicates that global educational systems are producing a global surplus of credentialed, skilled workers beyond current employment requirements, with the largest increases coming in developing economies such as China and India.[53] Globally, enrollments in higher education have doubled since the 1990s, from 76 million to an estimated 179 million in 2009.[54] China currently has more people enrolled in higher education than the United States and plans to add 95 million more graduates to its labor force by 2020.[55] The effect of this surge in global supply of educated labor has been to empower transnational capital to exploit a global "labor arbitrage" or "auction" for cut-rate low- and high-skilled labor (i.e. the race to the bottom) that has significantly eroded the bargaining power and repressed the wages of young workers with and without degrees.[56]

Keynesian economists argue that education is not the source of our problems and that generational precarity is actually contingent upon a broader set of issues rooted primarily in faulty ideology and policy failures. For instance, in his book *The Price of Inequality*, Joseph Stiglitz, former chief economist of the World Bank, condemns what he views as a new Gilded Age and points to a variety of intersecting trends generating grotesque levels of inequality and hardship for working people. This includes four decades dominated by supply-side rationalities and regressive tax policy that have precipitated steep cuts to public investments in infrastructure, education, and human services; deregulatory excesses leading to multiple speculative financial bubbles and busts; the decline of unions and the bargaining power of workers; soaring compensation for executives, hedge-fund managers, and bankers largely unrelated to productivity; and the domination of state policy by corporate-financial elites, who are increasingly unmoored from geographical constraints to capital mobility and production, and are therefore no longer as reliant on domestic markets, services, and workers (thus their primary aim is to socialize their costs and losses while keeping taxes and wages as low as possible).[57] As a result, according to Stiglitz, and despite the fact that the productivity of the average worker has slowly but steadily increased over the past four decades, economic gains and wealth have been upwardly distributed to the very top of the class structure. In the United States, for instance, 90 percent of the wealth produced over the past decade has accrued to the top 1 percent. This has done great damage to the economy and also the social fabric.

Recently Thomas Piketty, Emmanuel Saez, and Gabriel Zucman have further added to this picture. They observe that the bottom half of US households have only received 1 percent of the gains in economic growth over the past three decades.[58] At the same time, pre-tax income for this group has stagnated at $16,000 per household, adjusted for inflation. As middle- and working-class livelihoods have declined and precarity has expanded, one prominent consequence has been that households have been encouraged to take on increasing levels of consumer debt to make up the difference for stagnating wages and soaring cost of living, especially in housing, higher education, and health care (the number one cause of family bankruptcy in the US is an inability to service debt incurred through medical costs).[59] While consumer debt has functioned as a mode of what Colin Crouch has referred to as "privatized Keynesianism," it has also coincided with various structural instabilities including multiple speculative financial bubbles and busts, jobless recoveries, and anemic rates of economic growth.[60] The result has been a stunning expansion of economic insecurity and inequality, felt most keenly by the young.

Such precarious conditions create barriers to both educational and social development. Moderate neo-Keynesians such as Stiglitz and Paul Krugman advocate for rethinking public policy and reviving social-democratic New Deal progressivism in order to assuage inequality and precarity. They view such inequality and insecurity not only as a moral and policy problem, but also as a drag on economic productivity and growth that state intervention can resolve. This includes using the state to provide demand-side stimulus through progressive taxation, robust infrastructure spending, public investment in human services and education, and even direct public job creation. Their general prescription is therefore oriented to a new social policy compact that includes the extension of economic as well as civil and political rights to citizens. Krugman observes:

> If we want a society of broadly shared prosperity, education isn't the answer—we'll have to go about building that society directly. We need to restore the bargaining power that labor has lost over the last 30 years, so that ordinary workers as well as superstars have the power to bargain for good wages. We need to guarantee the essentials, above all health care, to every citizen. What we can't do is get where we need to go just by giving workers college degrees, which may be no more than tickets to jobs that don't exist or don't pay middle-class wages.[61]

Keynesian perspectives thus rightly reject the ideological claims of mainstream economists that, if left alone, capitalism naturally tends toward equilibrium and broadly distributed prosperity, particularly if educational systems continue to keep pace with technological change and development. They also recognize the inherently political nature of markets and the centrality of the state in providing the rules of the road for capital accumulation. However, Keynesians are primarily concerned with finding the right policy solutions to make capitalism "work" by generating effective demand. In other words, they assert that the disequilibrium tendencies of capitalism can be brought into equilibrium through enlightened use of state interventions. Generational precarity is here viewed primarily as a policy issue rather than as symptomatic of deeper conflicts located within the structural dynamics of capitalism as a system. Thus, like mainstream economic perspectives, Keynesians view the economic integration of the young through a technocratic lens. However, rather than looking to self-regulating markets and market-based educational logics of human-capital development as solutions to the crisis, they advocate for new regulatory mechanisms to stimulate growth and promote direct generation of employment through the state (which would also include training and retraining workers for new types of jobs demanded by technological change). Absent from both mainstream and Keynesian perspectives is any sense of how class relations (as a bundle of conflicts over financial, cultural, and social capital) and real historical political conditions (balance of these social and ideological forces in relation to the state and capital) function to shape the underlying dynamics of education and employment in relation to the inherent contradictions and structural tendencies of capitalism as a system.

Precarity as a Symptom of Systemic Crisis

In his landmark contribution, *Capital in the Twenty-First Century*, the French economist Thomas Piketty has contributed to reigniting a broader conversation about the long-run tendencies of capitalism.[62] Based on income-tax data covering two centuries and many nations, Piketty concludes that stagnation, precarious employment, and extreme concentrations of wealth are historical features of capitalism, rather than temporary deviations that self-regulating markets will eventually correct. The only way to manage and/or offset these tendencies in our present moment, Piketty argues, is either through massive capital devaluation, such as through war, or through some sort of quasi-Keynesian social-democratic compromise of global taxation and wealth redistribution.

Piketty's argument rests on the observation that when the rate of return on capital rents (profits, stocks, dividends, bonds, inherited wealth, etc.) exceeds the rate of growth ($r > g$), wealth concentrates in fewer and fewer hands. He suggests that the rate of return on capital has consistently exceeded rates of growth by 3–4 percent over the past two centuries. In our current period, as in the nineteenth century, the accumulated wealth of the top of the class structure largely results from inheritance of massive fortunes and returns on rent-seeking activities by the rich. Piketty also notes the rise of "super-managers" who have been enabled to set their own lavish compensation packages, wholly unrelated to actual contributions to economic productivity. These insights directly challenge ideological accounts by those such as Tyler Cowen that suggest we now live in a "hyper-meritocracy" in which those at the top are supposedly more virtuous, intelligent, and productive than the rest. Piketty refers instead to a new form of "patrimonial capitalism" ruled by a plutocratic class of rentiers and heirs who leverage their economic, cultural, and social capital to acquire and maintain unprecedented financial and political power.

Importantly, Piketty observes that education is indeed absolutely essential for promoting economic and social development, particularly in regions where education has historically been underdeveloped. However, at the same time, his analysis indicates that the expansion of inequality, and, by extension, generational precarity, cannot be reduced to differences in formal education and/or differences in productivity stemming from differential access and acquisition of human capital. Rather, the distribution of wealth, income, and economic security is located primarily within the historical dynamics of capitalism as well as in a neoliberal political order oriented to short-term, speculative rent-seeking and consolidated plutocratic decision-making. Thus in contrast to mainstream economic doctrine, which asserts self-regulating markets always tend toward equilibrium and prosperity for all, Piketty writes: "there is no natural, spontaneous process to prevent destabilizing, inegalitarian forces from permanently prevailing."[63]

Crucially here—and this is also a point long made by both Keynesians and Marxists—high levels of inequality are harmful not only to the promotion of educational and social development, but also to capitalism. As the rich tend to hoard their wealth, avenues for productive investment decline and the purchasing power to fuel growth is eroded. In venues such as the World Economic Forum meetings in Davos, Switzerland, these issues are increasingly and openly discussed by elites. For instance, Christine Lagarde, the former managing director of the International Monetary Fund, has called on elites to create a more "inclusive capitalism," to save capitalism from itself.[64]

Piketty is largely dismissive of Marx and therefore stays within the basic coordinates of institutional economics, albeit of a heretical strain. As a consequence Piketty generally avoids attempting to account for the structural contradictions of capitalism as a system. In contrast, the analytical value of Marxian perspectives is that they position generational precarity within a set of dynamics that reach beyond the surface of supply-and-demand frameworks orienting mainstream economics and Keynesian approaches. As such, they cast doubt on the capacity of either educational systems or state policy to maintain equilibrium under capitalism. Rather, education, employment, and state policy are viewed as reflective of irreconcilable conflicts and tensions. Foremost is the recognition that capitalism's own internal necessity to perpetually expand contains fundamental disequilibrium tendencies and barriers to growth that are internal to the "normal" functioning of the system. This stems from four basic features of capitalism:

1. *Capitalism is based on endless accumulation and growth.* This is characterized by and accomplished through the production and realization of surplus value (i.e. profit). Without perpetual growth there is no capitalism.
2. *Capitalism is based on an antagonistic relation between capital and labor.* This antagonism arises out of what Marx referred to as the "organic composition" of capital. This is composed of "constant

capital," or private ownership and investments in productive forces (plant, machinery, tools, etc), and "variable capital," which refers to wages allocated to labor. Profit reflects the gap between variable capital, or wages allocated, and the surplus value generated by labor in the production process. This surplus value is appropriated by capital as capital—a portion of which must be reinvested to support expansion of productive activities for endless accumulation, reinvestment, and growth.

3. *Capitalism is based on ruthless inter-firm competition.* This impels large businesses and corporations to always seek new ways of reducing their operating costs and increasing efficiency in production. They do so by seeking out the lowest possible wage for labor and through productivity-enhancing innovations, technologies, and organizational strategies. This allows capitalist firms to increase their market share and capture relative surplus value at the expense of competitors. The losers are ultimately either taken over and therefore absorbed by ever larger monopolistic competitors, or go bust.

4. *Capitalism requires maintaining a balance between expanded accumulation and a relative level of unemployment and precarious employment.* This is reflected in what Marx referred to as the 'reserve army' of workers. According to Marx, the circuits of capital accumulation tend to increase demand for labor as growth is stimulated and employers seek to expand production and hiring. However, if demand for labor rises too high, and too quickly, it empowers workers relative to capital and places upward pressure on wages, which can squeeze profits and ultimately threaten to bring capital accumulation to a standstill. The 1970s economic crisis of "stagflation" and the subsequent rejection of the postwar Keynesian compromise between capital and labor and turn to neoliberalism under Reagan and Thatcher in the 1980s is often attributed to such a "profit squeeze," brought on by the apparently "excessive" wage demands made by organized labor unions. The lesson, as similarly dictated by the demands of inter-capitalist competition, is that capital must constantly increase efficiencies within production,

typically through new technology, that displace workers and keeps them in a subordinate position. In this way, precarity is a necessary political strategy for capitalism, as capital requires insecure and surplus workers to compete against and hold down the wages of those actively employed. However, as capital attempts to minimize wages and maximize labor-saving efficiencies, what it saves in production comes back to haunt it at the moment of realization, as populations lack the purchasing power to fuel the consumption necessary to spur the endless compound growth demanded by capitalism.

David Harvey suggests that these features of capitalism are inherently contradictory, unstable, ever shifting, geographically contingent, interdependent, and conflict-ridden. Harvey argues that capitalist crises arise out of various types of potential barriers or antagonisms to the continuous realization of surplus value along the circuit of accumulation (M–C–M'). He lists eight such antagonisms that can disrupt accumulation:

> (1) inability to mass together enough original capital to get production under way (barriers to entry problems); (2) scarcities of labor or recalcitrant forms of labor organization that can produce profit squeezes; (3) disproportionalities and uneven development between sectors within the division of labor; (4) environmental crises arising out of resource depletion and land and environmental degradation; (5) imbalances and premature obsolescence due to uneven or excessively rapid technological changes driven by the coercive laws of competition and resisted by labor; (6) worker recalcitrance or resistance within a labor process that operates under the command and control of capital; (7) underconsumption and insufficient effective demand; (8) monetary and financial crises (liquidity traps) inflation or deflation, that arise within a credit system that depends on sophisticated credit instruments and organized state powers alongside a climate of faith and trust. At each one of these points internal to the circulation process of capital,

there exists an antinomy, a potential antagonism that can irrupt as an open contradiction.[65]

Any of these potential antagonisms can produce constraints to growth. However, as attempts are made to constantly expand productive potential there is a general tendency to generate excess productive capacity and excess capital relative to the available demand and reinvestment opportunities. Such crises of overaccumulation, Harvey argues, create situations in which surpluses of capital and surpluses of labor sit side by side with no clear way of reconnecting them. For instance, trillions in corporate profits sit on the sidelines or are sacked away in tax havens, with seemingly few avenues for profitable reinvestment in productive activities.[66] At the same time, growth continues to stall while the majority, and especially the young, confront stagnant wages and growing employment insecurity, debt, and income inequality, all of which place a further drag on economic growth.

In the 1980s and 1990s, the incorporation of vast cheap labor reserves and the opening of new markets through trade liberalization in Asia and across the Global South and the intensive movement of capital into ever riskier forms of deleveraging and financial speculation, combined with tax-cut stimuli and the extension of easy credit to middle- and lower-income consumers for houses and consumer goods, were able to offset these overaccumulation tendencies. John Bellamy Foster and Robert McChesney of the Monthly Review School argue, in their book *The Endless Crisis*, that such strategies appear exhausted as capital confronts new geographical (imperial), technological (innovative), and ecological (natural) barriers to expansion. After all, barring some unforeseen technological breakthroughs, how can a system based on endless expansion and exploitation of the natural environment be squared with finite planetary geography and natural resources? Bellamy Foster and McChesney suggest that limits to growth have impelled capital to become increasingly monopolistic and reliant on financial speculation; however, this contributes to new problems of stagnation and speculative instability. They observe that the consequences will disproportionately impact the next generation, represented symptomatically by the economic challenges facing youth across the world.

> The world economy as a whole is undergoing a period of slowdown. The growth rates for the United States, Europe, and Japan at the center of the system have been sliding for decades. In the first decade of this century these countries experienced the slowest growth rates since the 1930s; and the opening years of the second decade look no better. Stagnation is the word economists use for this phenomenon. In human terms it means declining real wages, massive unemployment, a public sector facing extreme budget crisis, growing inequality and a general and sometimes sharp decline in the quality of life. It produces all sorts of social and political crises, and these crises and their consequences will likely be the defining events of the coming generation.[67]

The central insight of Marxian crisis theory is that stagnation does not constitute an aberration, but is in fact the normal state of mature capitalist economies. Thus the brief period of rapid growth and near full employment in the postwar era in North America, Western Europe, and Japan during the so-called "golden age" of capitalism is to be viewed as an exception rather than a historical norm.[68] It was made possible largely by massive devaluation of capital during the war. However, as international competition began to mature in the late 1960s and 1970s the global economy began to revert to "normal" patterns of slow growth similar to that of the nineteenth century.[69] China and India are also recent examples of rapid economic growth, however significant barriers to long-term growth are now increasingly visible in both of these national contexts as well.

Generational precarity, in this frame, is not a temporary condition that self-regulating markets will simply correct, but potentially a long-term and chronic condition.

As Wolfgang Streeck and others within the tradition of political economy have detailed, without countervailing social forces and democratic pressures, unfettered capitalism tends to erode not only the social fabric, but also the basis of its own expansion and reproduction.[70] Moreover, when growth stalls and inequality increases, a cascading set of consequences follow that tend to be self-reinforcing—various fiscal crises of the state, expanding public and private debt, and intensifying social conflicts, including new expressions of state violence, racism, nativism, and ethnic chauvinism—all of which are being expressed in distinct ways in our own historical moment. This is not to say, of course, that something like racism can be reduced to either GDP and/or to social class, but rather that precarious conditions tend to heighten status anxieties and social tensions that can feed into and generate new forms of resentment, exclusion, violence, and "othering."

These issues are not simply economic in nature, but are rooted in *political conflicts* over the state as well as embedded historical, cultural, technological, and ideological relations and phenomena. Mainstream economists nonetheless continue to offer unfettered self-regulating markets, along with human-capital development through educational restructuring and the endless specter of deregulated speculative financial bubbles, as ways to stimulate growth and prosperity. Keynesians rightly reject austerity and support expanded government social investments to reduce inequality and stimulate employment. However, like the neoliberals, they never question the underlying logic of endless accumulation (no matter the social and ecological consequences) that make a return to golden-age Keynesian equilibrium and social security elusive, if not impossible. This is not to suggest that education and the progressive transformation of state policy are not crucial elements in addressing generational precarity. Indeed they are. However, countering generational precarity and promoting flourishing conditions for coming generations will require a much broader conversation and exercise of the creative social imagination.

Realizing alternative possibilities for the future of young people requires engaged contestations over ideology, which brings the question of education back into the discussion, but in a different frame. The ongoing effects of global financial instability stemming from the 2008 crisis have made contradictions within global capitalism, such as growing inequality and labor-market insecurity among the young, sharper and more visible. Such contradictions are readily apparent in the inadequacy of human-capital explanations for addressing generational precarity. Young people are here said to be either undereducated or overeducated in the wrong areas, requiring skill enhancement in technical fields, innovation, and entrepreneurialism. However, the reality is that the emerging *permanent crisis economy* may increasingly require a relatively small number of skilled technical workers, especially as advances in automation threaten to displace many job niches over coming decades. Moreover, as has been well documented in the sociology of education, inequalities and the instabilities that accompany poverty and economic insecurity erode the basis of educational development.[71] While education can indeed enhance innovation and workforce readiness (not to mention promote critical forms of culture, knowledge, and consciousness), and state policies can stimulate employment through various mechanisms, these strategies cannot resolve structural trends that are displacing jobs and destabilizing families and communities. We need to think far more creatively about the kinds of societies we want to live in—societies in which young people, workers, and the environment are subject to a relentless race to the bottom, or societies committed to secure, sustainable, and flourishing lives and livelihoods for all.

Notes

1. Guy Standing. *The Precariat: The New Dangerous Class*. A&C Black, 2011.
2. Brett Neilson and Ned Rossiter. "Precarity as a Political Concept, or, Fordism as Exception." *Theory, Culture & Society* 25, no. 7–8 (2008): 51–72.
3. On the empirical question of labor surpluses see Daniel Alpert. "Glut: The US Economy in the Age of Oversupply." *Third Way*, 2016. Retrieved from www.thirdway.org/report/glut-the-us-economy-and-the-american-worker-in-the-age-of-oversupply
4. World Bank Press Release. "Addressing the Youth Employment Crisis Needs Urgent Action." October 13, 2015. Retrieved from www.worldbank.org/en/news/press-release/2015/10/13/addressing-the-youth-employment-crisis-needs-urgent-global-action
5. Ibid.
6. Peter Coy. "The Youth Unemployment Bomb." *Bloomberg Businessweek*, February 2, 2011. Retrieved from https://www.bloomberg.com/news/articles/2011-02-02/the-youth-unemployment-bomb
7. Caelainn Barr and Shiv Malik. "Revealed: The 30-Year Economic Betrayal Dragging Down Generation Y's Income." *The Guardian*, March 7, 2016. Retrieved from https://www.theguardian.com/world/2016/mar/07/revealed-30-year-economic-betrayal-dragging-down-generation-y-income

8   Ibid.
9   Ibid.
10 Shahien Nasiripour. "3 Charts that Show Just How Dire the Student Debt Crisis has Become." *Huffington Post Business*, February 3, 2016. Retrieved from www.huffingtonpost.com/entry/3-charts-student-debt-crisis_us_56b0e9d0e4b0a1b96203d369
11 Laura Heck. "A Generation on Edge: A Look at Millennials and Mental Health." *Vox*, November 19, 2015. Retrieved from www.voxmagazine.com/news/features/a-generation-on-edge-a-look-at-millennials-and-mental/article_533c1384-fe5b-5321-84ae-8070ec158f17.html
12 Jesse Ferreras. "Millennials Working Longer than Full Time Hours in Numerous Countries: Study." *The Huffington Post*, June 2, 2016. Retrieved from www.huffingtonpost.ca/2016/06/02/millennials-work-longer-hours-manpower-study_n_10230268.html
13 Goran Therborn. *The Killing Fields of Inequality*. Malden, MA: Polity, 2011.
14 Jennifer Silva. *Coming Up Short*. Cambridge, MA: Harvard University Press, 2013, 27.
15 United States Government Accountability Office. "K-12 Education: Better Use of Information Could Help Agencies Identify Disparities and Address Racial Segregation." Retrieved from www.gao.gov/assets/680/676745.pdf
16 Richard Wilkinson and Kate Pickett. *The Spirit Level*. New York, NY: Penguin, 2009.
17 Sarah Ayres Steinberg. "America's 10 Million Unemployed Youth Spell Danger for Future Economic Growth." Center for American Progress, 2013. Retrieved from https://www.americanprogress.org/issues/economy/reports/2013/06/05/65373/americas-10-million-unemployed-youth-spell-danger-for-future-economic-growth/
18 Loic Wacquant. *Punishing the Poor: The Neoliberal Government of Social Insecurity*. Durham, NC: Duke, 2009.
19 Chris Sorenson. "The New Underclass: Why a Generation of Well-Educated, Ambitious, Smart Young Canadians Has No Future." *Maclean's*, January 16, 2013.
20 CBC. "Generation Jobless" (2013). Retrieved from www.cbc.ca/doczone/episodes/generation-jobless
21 OECD. "Education at a Glance" (2014). Retrieved from www.keepeek.com/DigitalAsset-Management/oecd/education/education-at-a-glance-2014_eag_highlights-2014en#page19
22 Anthony Carnevale and Stephen Rose. "The Undereducated American." Georgetown Public Policy Institute, 2011. Retrieved from http://cew.georgetown.edu/undereducated
23 David W. Livingstone. "Beyond Human Capital Theory: The Underemployment Problem." *International Journal of Contemporary Sociology* 36, no. 2 (1999): 163–192.
24 Raghuram Rajan. *Fault Lines*. Princeton, NJ: Princeton University Press, 2010, 8.
25 Claudia Goldin and Lawrence Katz. *The Race between Education, Technology, and Labor*. Cambridge, MA: Harvard University Press, 2008.
26 Ibid., 254.
27 David Autor. "The Polarization of Job Opportunities in the US Labor Market, Implications for Employment and Earnings." Center for American Progress and Brookings Institution: The Hamilton Project, 2010. Retrieved from https://economics.mit.edu/files/5554
28 David Autor and David Dorn. "How Technology Wrecks the Middle Class." *New York Times*, August 24, 2013.
29 Ibid.
30 Tyler Cowen. *Average Is Over: Powering America beyond the Age of the Great Stagnation*. New York, NY: Dutton, 2013, 3.
31 Ibid., 6.

32   Ibid., 4–6.
33   Ibid., 22–23.
34   Ibid.
35   David Brooks. "The Cost of Relativism." *New York Times*. March 15, 2015
36   Such views ignore capacious social science research that locates social fragmentation and family breakdown directly to the precariousness and extreme inequality characteristic of the post-industrial economy and the creation of economically redundant populations. See Therborn, 2011.
37   Cowen, 2013, 244–245.
38   John Maynard Keynes. *General Theory of Employment, Interest and Money*. New Delhi, India: Atlantic, 2006.
39   Keynes wrote: "The completeness of the [orthodox] victory is something of a curiosity and a mystery. It must have been due to a complex of suitabilities in the doctrine to the environment into which it was projected. That it reached conclusions quite different from what the ordinary uninstructed person would expect, added, I suppose, to its intellectual prestige. That its teaching, translated into practice, was austere and often unpalatable, lent it virtue. That it was adapted to carry a vast and consistent logical superstructure, gave it beauty. That it could explain much social injustice and apparent cruelty as an inevitable incident in the scheme of progress, and the attempt to change such things as likely on the whole to do more harm than good, commended it to the dominant social force behind authority." Keynes, 2006, 32–33.
40   Dean Baker. "Technology Didn't Kill Middle Class Jobs, Public Policy Did." *The Guardian*, November 26, 2013. Retrieved from https://www.theguardian.com/commentisfree/2013/nov/25/technology-middle-class-jobs-policy
41   Carl Benedikt Frey and Michael Osborne. "The Future of Employment: How Susceptible Are Jobs to Computerisation?" Retrieved from www.oxfordmartin.ox.ac.uk/downloads/academic/The_Future_of_Employment.pdf
42   National Employment Law Project. "Tracking the Low Wage Recovery: Industry Employment and Wages." 2014. Retrieved from www.nelp.org/publication/tracking-the-low-wage-recovery-industry-employment-wages/
43   Lawrence F. Katz and Alan B. Krueger. "The Rise and Nature of Alternative Work Arrangements in the United States, 1995–2015." *NBER Working Paper* no. 22667 (2016).
44   Jeff Madrick. "Education Is Not the Answer." *Harper's Magazine*, June 2013.
45   Heidi Shierholz, Natalie Sabadish, and Nicholas Finio. "The Class of 2013: Young Graduates Face Dim Job Prospects." Economic Policy Institute, 2013. Retrieved from: www.epi.org/publication/class-of-2013graduates job-prospects/
46   Steinberg, 2013.
47   Lawrence Summers. "The Economic Challenge of the Future: Jobs." *Wall Street Journal*, July 7, 2014. Retrieved from www.wsj.com/articles/lawrence-h-summers-on-the-economic-challenge-of-the-future-jobs-1404762501
48   Hal Salzman, Daniel Kuehn, and B. Lindsay Lowell. "Guestworkers in the High-Skill US Labor Market." Economic Policy Institute, Briefing Paper no. 359 (2013). Retrieved from www.epi.org/publication/bp359-guestworkers-high-skill-labor-market-analysis/
49   Ibid.
50   Ibid.
51   Ibid.
52   Peter Cappelli. *Why Good People Can't Get Jobs: The Skill Gap and What Companies Can Do about It*. Philadelphia, PA: Wharton Digital Press, 2012.
53   See Alpert, 2016.
54   Phillip Brown. "Education, Opportunity and the Prospects for Social Mobility." *British Journal of Sociology of Education* 34, no. 5–6 (2013): 678–700.

55 Ibid.
56 Phillip Brown, Hugh Lauder, and David Ashton. *The Global Auction: The Broken Promises of Education, Jobs, and Incomes*. Oxford, UK: Oxford University Press, 2010.
57 See Robert Reich. *Beyond Outrage: What has Gone Wrong with Our Economy and Our Democracy, and How to Fix It*. New York, NY: Vintage, 2012; Joseph E. Stiglitz. *The Price of Inequality: How Today's Divided Society Endangers our Future*. New York, NY: Norton, 2012.
58 Thomas Piketty, Emmanuel Saez, and Gabriel Zucman. "Economic Growth in the United States: A Tale of Two Countries." Washington Center for Equitable Growth, December 6, 2016. Retrieved from http://equitablegrowth.org/research-analysis/economic-growth-in-the-united-states-a-tale-of-two-countries/
59 Colin Crouch. "Privatized Keynsianism: An Unacknowledged Policy Regime." *British Journal of Politics and International Relations* 11 (2009): 382–399.
60 Kevin T. Leicht and Scott T. Fitzgerald. *Middle Class Meltdown in America: Causes, Consequences, and Remedies*. New York, NY: Routledge, 2013.
61 Paul Krugman. "Degrees and Dollars." *New York Times*, March 6, 2011. Retrieved from www.nytimes.com/2011/03/07/opinion/07krugman.html
62 Thomas Piketty. *Capital in the Twenty-First Century*. Cambridge, MA: Harvard University Press, 2014.
63 Ibid., 21.
64 Christine Lagarde. "Economic Inclusion and Financial Integrity." An Address to the Conference on Inclusive Capitalism, 2014. Retrieved from https://www.imf.org/external/np/speeches/2014/052714.htm
65 David Harvey. *A Companion to Marx's Capital: Volume 1*. New York, NY: Verso, 2010, 337–338.
66 See Stiglitz, 2012.
67 John Bellamy Foster and Robert McChesney. *The Endless Crisis*. New York, NY: Monthly Review Press, 2012, vii.
68 This is a point made with exceptional detail and clarity by James Galbraith. *The End of Normal*. New York, NY: Simon & Schuster, 2014.
69 See Robert Brenner. *The Economics of Global Turbulence*. New York, NY: Verso, 2006.
70 See Wolfgang Streeck. *How Will Capitalism End? Essays on a Failing System*. New York, NY: Verso, 2017.
71 See Wilkinson and Pickett, 2009.

4
CREATIVITY: EDUCATION AND THE COMMON

Creativity has emerged over the past two decades as a prominent theme in business, academic, and state policy discussions. Deployed under an umbrella of neologisms—"creative economy," "creative class," "creative age," "creative citizenship," "creative industries," and "creative cities"—creativity has been positioned as a key capacity for addressing the overlapping economic, technical, social, and environmental challenges of the twenty-first century. The rhetoric of creativity has also become prevalent within educational reform discussions where it has been geared toward promoting governmental, curriculum, and research initiatives aimed at spurring human capital formation, innovation, entrepreneurialism, and economic expansion over the coming decades.[1] From transnational organizations such as the World Bank, the OECD, and the United Nations, to mega-billionaire venture philanthropists such as Bill Gates and Eli Broad, to academics and journalists such as Richard Florida and Thomas Friedman, creativity has emerged as a dominant frame in efforts to imagine educational reform in K-12 and higher education that is responsive to an advanced global capitalism increasingly reliant on intellectual property and cognitive labor as engines of economic growth and financial valorization.

It is thus now widely recognized by academics, business leaders, policy makers, and economists that knowledge and creativity have become drivers of economic value within the global economy. As such, many argue that educational systems must become responsive to these trends. For some, the "creative economy" signals the possibility of greater openness and dynamism in educational systems and the development of more fluid and democratic educational structures modeled on network and digital infrastructures that can promote enhanced cooperation in knowledge production and the broad development of human capability and mass intellectuality. This chapter suggests that trends within educational policy and governance present distinct barriers for realizing such possibilities. It mobilizes autonomist conceptions of "cognitive capitalism," "biopolitical production," and the "common" as an analytic grammar for conceptualizing creativity as a material and discursive force at the center of current educational debates and conflicts over knowledge and subjectivity. While capitalism is increasingly dependent on analytical, cooperative, linguistic, affective, and inventive social capacities, or what can be called the common (the epistemological and ontological basis of creativity), neoliberal formations subvert the creative potential of education through strategies of privatization and control. Thus efforts to manage creativity in K-12 and higher education are ultimately unstable, revealing what the EduFactory Collective has referred to as the "double crisis" in education. This refers to the erosion of the social foundations of education conjoined with emergent crises within the creative and communicative circuits of cognitive labor and value as they intersect with educational processes. Ultimately, creativity rests at a key axis of contestation between state–corporate power and the possibility of imagining and calling into being alternative democratic and sustainable futures rooted in the common—which represents a struggle both of and for education.

System Crisis and Creative Economy

Capitalism is eminently creative. It is based on an imperative of unlimited expansion and the necessity to perpetually overcome its own internal and external limits. New outlets for profit have to be continuously found in order to ensure the generation and reinvestment of capital surpluses through forms of "creative destruction" in the opening of new markets; the geographic and institutional management of capital, labor, commodities, and information; and the integration of new models of financial innovation and investment. While capitalism is inherently dynamic, it is also intrinsically prone to instability and crisis. Contemporary ongoing instabilities in global markets, sovereign debt crises, and widespread austerity can be understood as an ongoing systemic crisis organizing new limitations and possibilities for capital. As David Harvey notes, "financial crises serve to rationalize the irrationalities of capitalism. They typically lead to reconfigurations, new models of development, new spheres of investment, and new forms of class power."[2]

The current crisis is rooted in the transition from the industrial-Fordist model of national production in the 1970s to post-Fordist globalization in the 1980s and 1990s. This historical turn has produced what Saskia Sassen has referred to as new "predatory formations" of global capitalism and elite wealth concentration built on a wave of privatization, wage repression (outsourcing, automation, free trade/labor zones, casualization, and precaritization), new informational and communicative processes, and speculative innovations and semiotic manipulations in the financial markets.[3] Combined with the rise of a deregulated "shadow-banking" sector, these developments have led to myriad structural instabilities and a ripple of bubbles and busts—East Asia 1997, Silicon Valley 2000–2001, Argentina 2001—culminating in the Wall Street crash in 2008 and the debt crisis and destabilization of Western Europe across the period 2009–2017.[4] The result has been a generalized expansion of inequality and instability. While the architects and cheerleaders of neoliberal globalization claimed that unbridled information-driven capitalism would usher in a new era of "friction-free" exchange in a "flat" world, everywhere we turn we seem to be confronted with new walls, hierarchies, and conflicts.

Out of this milieu, creativity has emerged as a central theme in debates over state restructuring and economic planning. The turn to creativity and creative economy can be understood to share a complicated genealogy with ideas associated with the "knowledge economy" and "information revolution". This includes perspectives on the "post-industrial society" articulated in distinct ways by Alain Touraine and Daniel Bell; the management theories of Peter Drucker; Alvin Toffler's "Third Wave" studies; the "knowledge society" popularized in the 1990s by Nico Stehr; Robert Reich's analysis of "symbolic analytic labor"; and analysis of digital network capitalism by Manuel Castells and Yochai Benkler.[5] While diverse in orientation and content, theories of the "knowledge economy" have tended to share certain consistencies in efforts to describe and imagine an informational phase of capitalist development characterized by more fluid and decentralized organizational forms and the spread of information technologies and information-driven regimes of production, work, finance, and culture across the globe.[6]

The rise of creative-economy discourse shares many characteristics of the "knowledge economy" theses. Since the late 1990s, business and policy makers have asserted the value of fostering what have become known as the "creative industries" defined by a widely cited Creative Industries Taskforce set up in the United Kingdom as "those industries which have their origin in individual creativity, skill and talent and which have a potential for wealth and job creation through the generation and exploitation of intellectual property."[7] The term "creative economy" has been used more recently by both John Howkins, in his book *How People Make Money from Ideas*, and in a series of books by Richard Florida, most notably *The Rise of the Creative Class*, to describe the centrality of creativity and ideas for economic development in spheres such as regional and urban planning, diversified commodity production and circulation, workforce development, institutional and network restructuring, media, and finance.[8]

In Florida's view, creativity is the "defining feature of economic life ... [It] has come to be valued—and systems have evolved to encourage and harness it—because new technologies, new industries, new wealth and all other good economic things flow from it".[9] Florida has boldly asserted that we have even entered a new historical phase, the "Creative Age," composed of "(1) new systems of technological creativity and entrepreneurship (2) new and more effective models for producing goods and services, and (3) a broad social, cultural and geographic milieu conducive to creativity of all sorts."[10] Hence there are myriad uses, meanings, and spheres that creativity encompasses and to which it is tasked. Matteo Pasquinelli usefully breaks down this "creative thing":

> Creative labour (as autonomous or dependent work), creativity as faculty and production, the creative product (with all its layers: hardware, software, knoware, brand, etc), the free reproducibility of the cognitive object, the intellectual property on the product itself, the social creativity behind it, the process of collective valorization around it. Moreover, the social group of creative workers (the "creative class" or "cognitariat"), the "creative economy" and the "creative city" represent further and broader contexts.[11]

Across these various sectors, creativity is positioned as an engine to expand economic innovation and valorization. In an economy where new sources of value and capitalist expansion have been heavily premised on privatization, intellectual property, and speculative finance, creativity becomes a key resource for the invention of new markets, products, and patterns of work and institutional management. On one level, creativity can be understood as a rhetorical figure in the deepening naturalization and enforcement of neoliberal governmentality and global capitalism. Former Microsoft CEO Bill Gates, for example, has named "creative capitalism" as a force to unite both global corporate expansion and altruism so as to ameliorate poverty and climate change through the further extension and intensification of market forces, competition, and global consumerism. However, elements of the "creative thing" cannot be reduced to the delusional thinking that endless commodification will save the world. Not only do the circuits of creative activity often refuse and work to challenge neoliberal economism, such as in the non-proprietary Open Source, P2P, or Creative Commons movements, but they also contain resistant grounds for generating spaces and circulations of social cooperation and democratic invention outside the disciplinary specters of capitalism and the state.

The creative economy can thus be read as a site of tension in the evolution of a global capitalism encountering new constraints and points of conflict. Undeniably, amid the intensification of global crises, creativity and mass intellectuality are indeed essential for imagining and realizing more sustainable and equitable futures. This raises fundamental questions, however. How can we understand the dynamics of creativity as a force of valorization and conflict within the contemporary moment? How does education as central node in the circuits of creativity, innovation, and knowledge production factor into these processes, particularly within the fields of educational policy and governance? How might an analysis of educational dynamics help us to answer the most pressing questions of all: What kind of creativity? In whose interests? And to what ends?

Toward an Analytic Grammar of Creativity

One of the most dynamic analyses of creativity in recent years has been derived from autonomist thought. Associated with thinkers such as Carlo Vercellone, Christian Marrazi, Paulo Virno, Franco "Bifo" Berardi, Mauricio Lazzarato, and Michael Hardt and Antonio Negri, autonomism is characterized by a recentering of the capital/labor relation within critiques of post-Fordist production and work through the reassertion of the creative and constitutive dimensions of human activity and resistance as it unfolds within capitalism.[12] This analysis has offered a kind of alternative genealogy and conceptual grammar from which to approach the knowledge-society and creative-economy theses.

Autonomists have argued that over the past four decades industrial capitalism has mutated in ways that privilege intellectual and communicative forms of labor and valorization. This theory of "cognitive capitalism" is derived from a reading of Marx's conception of the "general intellect" outlined in a section of the *Grundrisse* known as the "Fragment on Machines."[13] Here Marx speculates that future innovations contain the potential to pass a threshold whereby the collective knowledge embedded in machines—i.e. the "general intellect"—competes directly with physical labor as the primary driver of production and valorization. As he puts it, this occurs when "general social knowledge has become a direct force of production" and "the conditions of the process of social life itself have come under the control of the general intellect and have been transformed in accordance with it."[14] Carlo Vercellone has argued that the "hypothesis" of cognitive capitalism thus "cannot be reduced to the mere constitution of an economy founded on knowledge". Rather, as Marx's deeper formulation implies, it is "the formation of a knowledge-based economy framed and subsumed by the laws of capital accumulation."[15]

According to autonomist thinkers, cognitive capitalism signals the transformation of capitalism into a productive force at the level of knowledge, sociality, language, and communication. Michael Hardt and Antonio Negri have referred to this as "biopolitical production"—a term they derive from Michel Foucault's analysis of modern systems of power and governmentality.[16] They argue that biopolitical production has meant that "the traditional economic division between productive and reproductive labor breaks down ... as capitalist production is aimed ever more clearly at the production of not only (and perhaps not even primarily) commodities but also social relationships and forms of life."[17] According to Hardt and Negri, the *object* of production increasingly tends toward the production of a *subject*; that is, the general intellect, or what they simply refer to simply as the common—ideas, values, affects, data, code, images, and social relationships. "This means, of course, not that the production of material goods, such as automobiles and steel, is disappearing or even declining in quantity but rather that their value is increasingly dependent on and subordinated to immaterial factors and goods."[18] For instance, think here of the intensification of factory automation enabled by innovations in robotics and machine learning all powered by information software, or the evolution of just-in-time supply chains based on digital logistics integration, and/or the collective production of data through our online behavior and social-media participation that is then captured and transformed into targeted advertising and new product development. All reflect the centrality of the common to capital.

In his conversations with Antonio Negri, Cesare Casarino has defined the *common* in distinction to the *commons*. Whereas the *commons* has traditionally referred to commonly held wealth, land, and natural resources, the common is here understood as an infinite nonrepresentational force of communicative and cultural production, "namely, a common intellectual, linguistic, and affective capacity along with its appertaining forms of realization, circulation, and communication—or, in short, thought, language, and affect, in both their potential and actual aspects."[19] Casarino observes that while the common is increasingly central to capitalism, it is always in a position of partial exteriority and autonomy from it. In other words, while capitalism may require the common as site of economic valorization, the common does not require capitalism.

As Carlo Vercellone and other economists have pointed out, cognitive capitalism relies on the expropriation of value from the common as "rent"—sometimes called "the becoming rent of profit." First, the becoming rent of profit refers to how, in a neoliberal context of stagnation and austerity, expropriation of value has become dependent on the commodification of formerly socialized goods, or what David Harvey calls "accumulation by dispossession"—i.e. the privatization and marketization of public assets such as schools, universities, transportation systems, hospitals, as well as natural resources and biogenetic materials such as seeds used in agriculture.[20] Second, at a deeper level, as Hardt and Negri's formulation of biopolitical production implies, what is increasingly at stake is the capture of value from the social production of the *common*. However, importantly, there are always aspects of the common—ideas, creativities, and affects—that *remain external* to systems of commodification and appropriation. This formulation raises a central contradiction within cognitive capitalism.

Knowledge, for instance, particularly within digital networks that allow for instant and infinite reproduction at zero cost, does not conform to traditional laws of production or scarcity. Instead knowledge becomes part of a digital commons of open access and abundance. Moreover, knowledge is enhanced and becomes more dynamic as it freely circulates and as individuals enter into cooperative arrangements of communication and exchange. An axis of struggle and crisis emerges here as capitalism attempts to organize systems to extract value from the common such as through privatization, paywalls, and legal architectures. In turn, these systems become a fetter to creativity and the social production of potentially valuable knowledge that emerges through exchange. Put differently, in its efforts to control and capture creative value as profit and to privatize knowledge as property, capital mobilizes apparatuses of organization and control such as patent monopolies and intellectual-property regimes that place limits on the free circulation of knowledge and thus the productivity and creative potential of the common.

A number of writers, including Hardt and Negri, have zeroed in on this contradiction to argue that the common is slowly undermining capitalism due to the digital abundance of knowledge and network "sharing" platforms based on the common that challenge or evade traditional proprietary arrangements and profit models (however minimally at the present time), such as open-source software, crowdsourcing, Creative Commons licensing, 3-D printing, sharing platforms such as Airbnb, and alternative crypto-currencies like Bitcoin.[21] Michael Hardt has argued that these developments signal an emerging site of conflict in the biopolitical economy: "as the common is corralled as property, the more its productivity is reduced; and yet expansion of the common undermines the relations of property in a general and fundamental way."[22]

Whether or not we agree that new forms of digital technology and centrality of knowledge are necessarily undermining, or pushing beyond, capitalism, autonomist perspectives offer an analytical grammar useful for thinking about creativity and education. The common can be understood as the immanent terrain of creativity. In this sense, creativity is what is proper to the common—a shared capacity for social invention, intellectuality, and collaboration that is embedded within yet always exceeds capture and control. Moreover, as capital seeks to control and expropriate the fruits of creativity on the basis of the common, it risks stifling creativity, and thus the well of valorization and innovation itself. Creativity thus represents a stubborn surplus and site of struggle within the communicative vectors of cognitive capitalism and neoliberal governmentality.

Creativity and Conflict in the EduFactory

The scholarly and activist network known as the EduFactory has insightfully argued that education has become a crucial site where the current contradictions of cognitive capitalism are expressed and mediated.[23] Its principal thesis is: "as once was the factory, so now is the university." If the factory was the archetypal institution of the Fordist industrial period oriented to production for national spaces of work and consumption, within the post-Fordist knowledge economy this is the university, with its cosmopolitan ambitions of production of knowledge and intellectual labor for globally dispersed networks.

Of course, one should be clear that schools and universities do not function exactly like industrial factories. Rather, they represent a site for the organization of the common, and thus embody generative tensions over knowledge and forms of labor and value privileged in contemporary capitalism. Formal education has, of course, always been implicated in the reproduction of class society and its racial and gendered hierarchies. However, K-12 and higher education have also provided an important sphere for social development and expansion of democratic imagination and social relations.

If we take autonomist hypotheses seriously, then calls for creativity within education speak to what the EduFactory calls the "double crisis." First, this refers to the evolving crisis of educational systems resulting from the neoliberal erosion of their social, intellectual, and cultural foundations. Second, it refers to the crisis specific to cognitive labor and value as they intersect with education organization and policy. Both sides of the double crisis represent conflicts over the common, between economic rationality on the one hand and the vitality of mass intellectuality on the other. The effect has been to place restrictions on those forms of education conducive not only to achieving progressive aims of enhancing freedom and equality, but also to capitalist valorization, as the social basis, creativity, and potentiality of education is diminished.

Building on the EduFactory's analysis, we might suggest that the double crisis can be understood through four interrelated frames. First, it is *global*. It is articulated and experienced in highly differentiated ways within and between transnational, national, regional, and metropolitan contexts. Educational sectors are in the position of reacting to as well as shaping new global economic and political realities, including the mediation and transformation of economic relations and institutions, temporalities of work and culture, and new articulations of centers/peripheries and social inclusions/exclusions. Second, it speaks to new *strategies of management*, as educational sectors have adopted and even in some cases pioneered their own market-based organizational forms. Within this schema, lines between the public and private blur as corporate and educational synergies generate new systems of measurement, auditing schemes, performance evaluations, curricular and research metrics, and labor controls so as to enhance the generation and capture of economic value from educational processes. This has coincided with qualitative shifts in the value of knowledge within educational spheres and a dominant emphasis on the input and output binaries of human-capital theory and its focus on entrepreneurialism and economic competition. Third, the double crisis is *economic* and *ongoing*. The persistence of labor precaritization and widening chasms in income and wealth inequality, along with widespread disinvestments in social infrastructures, including public schools and universities at all levels, points to the continued salience of the global economic crisis and speaks to its durability. This has made *adaptation* to crisis and its basis in deregulated bubble economics and austerity a lasting form and *new technique of governance*. Fourth, and on this later point, the double crisis is driving new arrangements of *power* and *stratification* that are constructing new hierarchies and social conflicts within and across what the EduFactory calls the "planetary educational market."

While the EduFactory project concentrates its analysis on the university, I would like to suggest that the double crisis also resonates with K-12 education in distinct ways. In what follows, I situate creativity in K-12 and higher education within the context of the double crisis at the level of social stratification, knowledge, and subjectivity.

Draining the Common in K-12 Education

In the aftermath of the global financial crisis of 2008, *New York Times* columnist Thomas Friedman wrote a piece entitled "The New Untouchables" in which he suggested that an "educational breakdown on Main Street" was the true underlying cause of US economic instability and the decline of the middle and working class.[24] Surveying the realities of a present and future labor market rooted in mobile networks of global production and information technology, the rise of China and India as strategic competitors, and the centrality of cognitive labor and creativity in driving economic growth, he suggested that without a "reboot" of the educational sector, many, if not most, American workers will be left behind. For Friedman, the educational challenge of the twenty-first century is to produce workers who possess "the imagination to make themselves untouchables"—that is, subjects who can invent the products, services, technologies, and employment niches of the future. He states that "schools have a doubly hard task now—not just improving reading, writing and arithmetic but entrepreneurship, innovation and creativity."

Friedman is far from alone here. Recent books such as *Out of Our Minds: Learning to Be Creative*, by Ken Robinson; *A Whole New Mind: Why Right-Brainers Will Rule the World*, by Daniel Pink; *A New Culture of Learning: Cultivating the Imagination for a World of Constant Change*, by Douglas Thomas and John Seely Brown; and *Creating Innovators: The Making of Young People Who Will Change the World*, by Tony Wagner, each express similar views, arguing that schools must promote imagination and creativity in the interest of economic growth so as to resolve the problems of the twenty-first century.[25] This conjuncture of creativity and creative labor has not been lost on the corporate world either. For instance, the Partnership for 21st Century Skills (now the Partnership for 21st Century Learning) was set up in the United States in 2002 as an educational advocacy group made up of a consortium of corporate entities and leaders from the media, technology, and education sectors such as AOL-Time Warner, Apple, CISCO Systems, Dell, Microsoft, Walt Disney, Oracle, McGraw-Hill, and Pearson. It argues for the integration into schools of market-driven twenty-first-century skills such as "creativity, innovation, critical thinking and financial, economic, business and entrepreneurial literacy."[26]

On the surface, these calls for more creativity, entrepreneurialism, and innovation would appear to recognize and support substantial investments in public K-12 education. If the creative economy demands fresh thinking about workforce capacities and open and dynamic institutions, then it might follow that the rhetoric of creativity would translate into a more expansive view of schooling as a site of social investment, intellectual engagement, and creative learning. If cognitive capitalism is oriented to generating value from the common—that is, from creativity and mass intellectuality—logically it would seem that calls for twenty-first-century skills would support an expansive view of public education based in commitments to human development and progressive pedagogy, while working to promote equity and autonomy. The reality has been somewhat different.

Taking the United States as our example, national concerns over public schooling and global economic competiveness are, of course, far from new. They became particularly salient during the Cold War and more recently intensified under the historical emergence of globalization and neoliberalization in the 1980s and 1990s. The Reagan-era task force and report entitled *A Nation at Risk* offered perhaps the paradigmatic statement on national anxieties over public educational performance in the emerging global economy: "If an unfriendly foreign power had attempted to impose on America the mediocre educational performance that exists today, we might well have viewed it as an act of war."[27] Here informative distinctions can be made between the liberal Keynesian rationalities that marked educational planning during the Cold War era and the past three decades of neoliberal policy incursions into the educational sphere. The Cold War era was marked by robust federal and state commitment to public funding and expanded educational access. While embedded within a clear-cut Fordist division of labor and a gendered and racialized social hierarchy, investments in public schooling combined with anti-poverty programs and a strong public ethos that emerged out of the social struggles of the 1960s, such as black freedom movements, feminist struggles, and anti-war movements, contributed to a dramatic reduction in educational and social inequalities, while creating (despite its many flaws) the most dynamic and accessible system of public education in world history. In contrast, the neoliberal revolution and extensive corporate involvement in public policy over the past four decades has led to the retrenchment of educational investment and the radical expansion of social and education inequality. As Michael Hardt has noted, "if the launch of Sputnik made the United States smarter, the attacks of September 11th, perceived as the primary challenge to the national position in this period, only made the country more stupid."[28] Permanent "war on terror," combined with the neoliberal revolution and extensive right-wing attacks on public schools and universities, has led to social disinvestment, accompanied by a narrowing of educational purpose co-extensive with market-driven corporate and financial interests.

Since the 1980s and 1990s, in the sphere of US elementary and secondary education policy, there has been an intensive and extensive path taken toward market integration and corporate management. First, this has meant widespread privatization efforts in the form of voucher initiatives and charter schools, as well as growing experiments in for-profit models of schooling. Second, along with privatization, the management of US schooling has been captured by technocratic logics that have sought to bring market-based strategies of accountability and institutional "efficiency" into schooling at all levels. This has included the standardization of curricula, the proliferation of auditing and evaluation mechanisms that tend to limit the professional autonomy of teachers, and an expansive emphasis on the rote learning of "basic skills" conjoined with incessant high-stakes standardized testing. These policies of privatization, standardization, and test-based accountability have been driven by an interconnected web of venture philanthropies such as the Gates and Walton foundations, free-market think tanks such as the Heritage Foundation and American Enterprise Institute, Wall Street firms such as Goldman Sachs, corporate and right-wing lobbying groups such as the American Legislative Exchange Council, media corporations such as Rupert Murdoch's News Corp (which owns Fox News), and neoliberal politicians across the Democratic and Republican parties. The corporate reform of public schools has been codified into law through George W. Bush's No Child Left Behind legislation and the Obama-era Race to the Top and Common Core State Standards.[29]

Far from promoting educational investments rooted in creativity and the general intellect, these policies have been more likely to "drain the common" than to nurture and expand it. First, in the name of creativity, freedom from state bureaucracy, and choice for parents, privatization has enabled the transfer of public assets over to publicly unaccountable private entities largely through the proliferation of charter schools, even though research is overwhelmingly clear that charters do not "perform" any better on average than traditional public schools. On a structural level, privatization has siphoned funding from public schools, leading to their further decline, and has often contributed to creating more, not less, inequality within districts. Moreover, the charter sector has been plagued by scandals and profiteering. For instance, 80 percent of charter schools in the state of Michigan are directly run for profit, and these schools have a dismal record of corruption and mismanagement.[30] For-profit charter schools operate by skimming off public tax dollars that are earmarked for classrooms, in the form of profits for corporate management companies and Wall Street investors. Problems in the charter sector are hardly confined to Michigan, either, as cases of rampant fraud and dysfunction have been uncovered in Ohio, Louisiana, Pennsylvania, Florida, and many other states.[31] Although one can certainly find creative charter schools based on progressive principles and models, there are now countless charters and corporate charter chains, such as Eva Muskowitz's celebrated Success Academies in New York, that are grounded in abhorrent authoritarian practices at odds with decades of social science on how children actually learn, thrive, and develop.[32]

Second, the expansion of corporate managerialism, standardized curriculum, and high-stakes testing has led to the narrowing of curriculum, the de-professionalization of teachers, and the marginalization of liberal arts subjects. High levels of teacher attrition (statistics suggest as many as three in every five new teachers leave the field in the first five years) can be attributed to constant attacks on teaching as a profession and the drive to control teachers' work and evaluate teachers by test score, even though test scores consistently reflect socioeconomic inequalities rather than teacher quality.[33] The testing and scripted-curriculum fetish is, of course, most zealously enforced in schools that serve low-income youth, where learning increasingly resembles what Paulo Freire described as "banking education"—the technical delivery of knowledge as an inert and lifeless object detached from the world and the subjective experiences of youth.[34] Such a reductive and mechanical approach to teaching and learning based only in quantification, measurement, objective metrics, and testing is detached from deeper ethical and intellectual considerations of knowledge construction, cooperation, dialogue, and exploration within the curriculum. It also becomes self-justifying and self-perpetuating. Linda McNeil refers to this as the "contradictions of control," whereby the implementation of market-based and standardized systems of management and accountability serve to reproduce their own logic.[35] For instance, low test scores become a justification for more testing and further efforts to control teaching and learning. Concurrently, high test scores are a sign that incessant testing is the key to improving performance on the tests. The problem of education within neoliberal management logic is thus always framed as never enough control, never enough measurement, never enough standardization, never enough testing.[36]

Third, privatization and test-based accountability exacerbate underlying sociological problems of inequality. In 2013, a threshold was passed whereby 51 percent of students in public schools in the US became classified as low-income or in poverty.[37] Sean Reardon at Stanford has documented that as inequality has rapidly expanded in the United States (the US has far higher rates of inequality and child poverty than any other affluent society, with nearly one in four children growing up in poverty), the income-achievement gap between affluent and poor kids has grown by 40 percent since 1980, signaling that privatization, standardization, and high-stakes testing have done nothing to staunch disparities in educational efficacy and outcomes, which are primarily rooted in the class and racial structure of US society rather than the relative "quality" of public schools.[38] For instance, on the PISA international comparison, US schools with a poverty rate of less than 10 percent scored higher than any other affluent nation on reading; schools with a 25 percent poverty rate or less were ranked third, and schools with a 75 percent poverty rate scored second to last.[39] Rather than seek to directly address social inequality and child poverty, while simultaneously developing *public schools as a common(s)* to serve all youth equitably in order to develop creativity and mass intellectuality, the neoliberal restructuring of education has contributed to transforming US schooling into an emerging three-tiered system—a small number of exclusive, mainly private schools to serve the rich; a middle tier made up largely of charter schools and more affluent public schools to train an increasingly insecure cadre of future middle-class service workers and professionals; and a strata of public schools at the bottom of the racial and socioeconomic hierarchy forming little more than testing warehouses and/or potential markets for educational speculators.

Ultimately, neoliberal policies of privatization and managerialism have tended to extend some of the worst aspects of industrial schooling, while pioneering new mechanisms of technocratic governance implicated in deepening social stratification and inequality. To take one example, the 400,000 students in the Chicago Public Schools system, almost 90 percent of whom are either African American or Latino/a and more than 90 percent of whom live at or below the federal poverty line, typically receive half the funding per year than their mostly white, middle-class, suburban counterparts receive. This means, for instance, that a group of 6,413 students who started elementary school in Evanston in 1994 and graduated from high school in 2007 had about $290 million more spent on their education than the same number of Chicago Public Schools students.[40] Furthermore, the schools attended by low-income and racially marginalized youth in Chicago are often in dismal states of repair, have bloated class sizes, are subject to mindless scripted curricula, and are increasingly materially and symbolically conjoined to the criminal justice system. Children of the elite, of course, can still expect a well-funded and enriching education that includes exploratory learning, small class sizes, interesting projects, and ample time for creative arts, while public schools for the majority are redefined within a standardized and market-driven framework of educational value as well as narrow conceptualizations of learning that capture and contain the educational commons rather than enhancing it.

Without major resistance, this process of eroding the educational common(s) in US schooling is likely to intensify in the years ahead, albeit within a theocratic bent, under the new Trump administration. The US Secretary of Education at the time of writing, Betsy DeVos, is a market fundamentalist and religious zealot who does not believe in science, expertise, knowledge, separation of church and state, or even universal education as a basic human right. She is committed to totally dismantling public schools through for-profit models.[41] This is hardly a recipe for producing a society of creative twenty-first-century workers, much less a society of flourishing human beings endowed with the creativity and agency necessary to meaningfully intervene in the world.

The market-driven and technocratic view of public education promoted by DeVos is widely shared by a new generation of corporate education reformers and educational entrepreneurs. On the one hand, there is a broad affirmation of non-instrumental capacities such as creativity and imagination typically associated with progressive modes of teaching and learning. On the other hand, there is a profound negation of the development and dynamic potentiality of these capacities as public education is radically defunded and the value and substance of learning are reconceived in purely instrumental terms (human capital, measurement, testing, etc). Thus the rhetoric of creativity as a modality of twenty-first-century schooling does not generally extend beyond market rationalities or values, representing a myopic vision of knowledge and learning as static abstractions detached from social context and deeper forms of intellectual and ethical development.

Neoliberal education rhetorically embraces creativity as a means to produce subjects capable of generating new economic value. However, the social dimensions of creativity are ignored, as creative value is reduced to a reductive economic vision of entrepreneurialism, technical knowledge, and subjectivity. This narrow rendering of creativity lends itself to education policies that stifle the development of social capacities and deeper ethical development of persons in educational contexts. Learning becomes little more than a prescriptive process of "content delivery" and testing. This is learning as a transmission of "units" of standardized knowledge, rather than a social process that is open-ended, dialogical, historically contingent, and grounded in the ethical, political, and cultural relations that are shaping the future. Ultimately, calls for creativity as economic ideology are blind to the reality that neoliberal education reforms *consistently fail on their own terms*—they do not produce the kinds of imaginative learning practices and social capabilities said to be required for capital accumulation in the biopolitical economy, nor do they advance autonomy and equity. In short, they stifle the common.

Managing Creativity in the Corporate University

Over the past decade, the University of Toronto embarked on a $200 million-dollar expansion of its Rotman School of Business. The new Rotman houses a much ballyhooed "Integrative Thinking Center," along with the "Martin Prosperity Institute," as well as the creativity guru himself, Richard Florida, who claims that the new business school "will reflect the 'new way to think' that is the basis of our approach, providing students, researchers, staff and the local community with a springboard to harness their creative capabilities." This serves a larger mission of "reinventing management tools and frameworks for a creative society."[42] With the Rotman expansion we get a glimpse of how creativity speaks to a reinvention of management that places business at the heart of a project to reframe the value and purpose of knowledge in the university. This is representative of how the university has more broadly responded to its role as a crucial node in cognitive capitalism's circuits of value. The contemporary university provides a key training and disciplinary ground for future knowledge workers and functions as key public infrastructure for generating and capitalizing on intellectual property, and also for publicly subsidizing corporate technological innovation. Out of the deregulatory and "new managerial" fever of the 1980s and 1990s has emerged what Nick Dyer-Witheford has referred to as "Corporate U." This is a university reconfigured in the image of the corporation and organized in accordance with corporate logics and business imperatives.[43]

The triumph of neoliberal ideology and values in the restructuring of higher education has produced a variety of well-documented trends. In his book *How the University Works*, Marc Bousquet incisively documents the recalibration of higher education's institutional and administrative norms under the neoliberal logic of "total quality management."[44] This has contributed to the radical casualization of university labor and erosion of the tenure system; the proliferation of standardization, audits, and evaluations in line with corporate managerialism; the rise of predatory for-profit colleges; the integration of profitable online and distance "learning" within traditional institutions; enhanced corporate university partnerships and the sinking of vast sums of money into business, bio-tech, pharmaceutical, energy, and military/defense research. Programs without direct application to industry have been subject to cuts, while budgets and resource allocation have become increasingly linked to economic outcomes. Within this schema students are increasingly configured as potential customers, debtors, consumers encouraged to pursue higher education as a form of economic credentialing, networking, and status distinction rather than as a means of humanization and the pursuit of knowledge and critical citizenship. Professors, or at least those 25–30 percent still fortunate enough to inhabit a tenure track, are imagined as the ultimate cognitive workers, less public intellectuals than entrepreneurial information delivery "technicians" and/or "producers." Meanwhile, university administration increasingly grows and leverages its position to attract corporate dollars and to capitalize on copyright, licensing, branding, and intellectual property. This has occurred at the same time that public funding to universities has been steadily declining, while university administration has presided over extensive tuition hikes, passing on the costs of new business parks and sports facilities and their own ballooning salaries through massive increases in financialized student debt.

Christopher Newfield has highlighted the contradiction between these trends and the demands of cognitive capitalism. He asks why it is that leaders in the United States and in other wealthy countries are "containing and cheapening the research and educational systems on which they say the future of their economies depend"—isn't this counterproductive for innovation and knowledge production in the creative economy?[45]

Newfield offers a sophisticated response to this question. He argues that cognitive capitalism is defined by a "productive contradiction" between the expropriation of value from the common and the "full knowledge that it is forcing knowledge out of its creative collective habitat."[46] Drawing on the management theory of Thomas Stewart, Newfield argues that cognitive capitalism has devised systems of knowledge management (KM) that enforce strict multi-layered controls over knowledge production and knowledge work. These systems rely heavily on complex arrangements of stratification within and between higher education and corporate capitalism in order to ensure the generation and value of proprietary knowledge even at the expense of placing limits on creativity and innovation.

The primary aim of KM is thus control, rather than creativity. For instance, Newfield observes there are roughly seven million STEM jobs in the US. This is a notoriously stratified sector that includes armies of precarious and subcontracted "permatemps" and "cognitariat" workers that perform most routine tasks without job security and benefits. This leaves a select few to perform the hardcore creative, technical, design, and conceptual work required for capitalization projects. Moreover, with 2.3 million higher-education degrees awarded each year in all fields, over a 30-year period (the length of a typical career) the university system produces roughly ten times more graduates than are required in the technical workforce. "The issue for knowledge industries then, is *not* how they can create armies of knowledge workers. The issue is the opposite: how can they limit their numbers and manage their output?"[47] Newfield suggests that the contradiction between rhetoric of twenty-first-century education for creativity and the neoliberal management, privatization, and defunding of public higher education comes into focus:

> The contradiction exists only if we assume that today's leaders of the knowledge economy actually seek a mass middle class, desire high standards of living for the vast majority of their population, and believe that the knowledge economy needs armies of college graduates. If instead, we posit that the political and business leaders of the knowledge economy seek a smaller elite of knowledge-based star producers, then the unceasing cheapening of public higher education in the U.S. and elsewhere makes more sense.[48]

Elites, of course, no longer require a robust public sphere. They can bypass the public altogether through private purchase of education, health care, transportation, and gated real estate. Elites and corporations are also less reliant on domestic labor markets within a global economy with increasing numbers of low- and high-skilled workers emerging from expanding global higher education. This may partially explain why elites have abandoned public investment in universal education in favor of privatization and training. In his book *Unmaking the Public University*, Newfield expands on these insights by outlining their historical, cultural, and political underpinnings.[49] He details how the rise of the post-industrial knowledge economy in the 1980s and 1990s corresponded to an intensification of conservative and right-wing attacks on the university. Such attacks on multiculturalism, postmodernism in the humanities, identity politics, political correctness, and affirmative action have ultimately eroded support for robust public funding and broad commitments to liberal arts and equitable access to public higher education. Moreover, they have fed into a culture of resentment among an insecure and beleaguered white middle class regarding a perceived loss of social status and the supposed advantages accrued to minority populations in the wake of the civil rights and feminist movements. For instance, it is now widely believed that racial and ethnic minorities are the overwhelming (and undeserving) beneficiaries of scholarships at US post-secondary institutions, when in reality, as the research of Mark Kantrowitz shows, minorities receive a much lower percentage of scholarships and grants across the United States than whites do.[50] Caucasian students receive 72 percent of all scholarships, but only make up 62 percent of the population. Minority students receive only 28 percent of all scholarships, while making up 42 percent of the population. White women have historically received the highest number of affirmative-action scholarships. Other signs of how the politics of white economic grievance have been channeled into racial resentment can be found in the widespread condemnation of campus protests affiliated with the Black Lives Matter movement and the normalization of white nationalist views on campuses and neo-fascist speakers such as Jared Taylor, Milo Yiannopoulos, and Richard Spencer, who coined the term alt-right.

Racial politics have functioned as a wedge, eroding support for public higher education among elites and the white middle class while promoting neoliberal logics of meritocracy and fantasies of a color-blind post-racial society that do not accord to sociological reality. This has hurt the middle and working class across the lines of race and ethnicity not only economically, but also intellectually and culturally, as solidarities have weakened and neoliberal ideology reconfigures sociality as cutthroat competition among isolated individuals. Newfield notes that "the culture war strategy" has functioned as a kind of "intellectual neutron bomb, eroding the social and cultural foundations of a growing, politically powerful, economically entitled, and racially diversifying middle class, while leaving its technical capacities intact."[51] The culture war, right-wing attacks on the university as a public sphere and bastion of multiculturalism and liberalism, deepening consumer values and identification, and the waning of liberal arts can thus be viewed as aspects of an "economic war," in the sense that these processes have reduced the institutional capacities of the middle and working class to grapple with changing historical conditions in non-market terms, and thus to imagine and advocate a framework from which to advance egalitarian social development across class and racial lines.

As Wendy Brown has argued, one of the principal casualties of the neoliberalization of higher education has been the decline of liberal arts as a basis for social and civic literacy and a precondition for democracy as a form of collective self-rule. The "status of liberal arts is eroding from all sides," she writes; "cultural values spurn it, capital is not interested in it, debt-burdened families anxious about the future do not demand it, neoliberal rationality does not index it, and, of course, states no longer invest in it."[52] The *post-social university* is gradually configured as little more than a mechanism for imparting twenty-first-century skills, a means of purchasing symbolic distinction in the form of credentials, and as a site for building one's portfolio value of human-capital stocks to be traded for jobs and money. What is lost is a deeper commitment to the forms of knowledge and consciousness necessary for production of social cooperation, creativity, and mass intellectuality in order to apprehend what is unique about this historical conjuncture and also to imagine futures beyond those captured by market logics. In a particularly conspicuous example of this logic, in 2015, Wisconsin governor Scott Walker proposed removing phrases in the University of Wisconsin mission statement such as "the search for truth," "public service," and "improve the human condition," and replacing them with the bluntly unedifying phrase "meet the state's workforce needs."[53]

All this is not to argue that education should not be connected to the question of livelihoods. Rather, within a historical moment at which a small number of secure livelihoods are available for an insecure middle and working class, the liberal arts become even more indispensable, not simply as a means of producing better workers for the creative economy (after all, the liberal arts are a principal means of producing people with the analytical, creative, cooperative, and affective sensibilities supposedly required within cognitive capitalism), but also as a foundation for a democratic politics and the modes of social responsibility and imagination necessary to redefine labor and value in the twenty-first century to ensure security, freedom, and equality for all. The role of the liberal arts and higher education is one of humanization, where circulation of values and visions of a life in common might develop beyond what David Graeber refers to as the "dead zones of the imagination" accompanying the dismal calculus of endless marketization of social life.[54]

Reclaiming Creativity for Educational Commons

Within K-12 and higher education, the concept of creativity is marked by instability and contradiction. Invocations to unleash creativity and innovation in educational contexts appear to stand in tension with the realities of the reorganization of education along the lines of privatization, audits and testing, standardization, and the marginalization of the social sciences and the humanities—processes that place limits on knowledge production and the free and cooperative exchange of ideas. One question that this raises is whether cognitive capitalism in fact requires a highly educated and mass creative workforce at all—requiring instead a very small and manageable core of cognitive workers. There is certainly a broad spectrum of evidence regarding deepening social stratification and insecurity across educational and employment sectors to support this conclusion.

An accompanying hypothesis might be that neoliberal educational management and policy have tended to mistake or misrecognize the educational capacities necessary for the biopolitical economy, taking entrepreneurial and technocratic knowledge and subjectivity for multifaceted and cooperative forms of innovative potential and creative value. If, indeed, cognitive capitalism tends to increasingly generate value from social processes on the basis of the common, and these processes are increasingly autonomous from capital and reliant on creativity, then the paradox emerges that I have tried to provisionally trace out in this chapter whereby tendencies in educational management and policy place restrictions and limitations on creativity, and hence on capital's own drive to economic value. This is indicative of what the Edu-factory has identified as the double crisis—the erosion of the social and intellectual foundations of public education due to the intensive and extensive application of economic and technocratic reason, and the attendant crisis in cognitive labor and value as it intersects with these processes.

There is another explanation to consider here, however, and it is one that I think is particularly important when considering the emancipatory and indeed *creative power* of education and knowledge as social and democratic forces. Perhaps, ultimately, linking creativity back to educational and social investments, expanded and equitable access, and broad, open, and interdisciplinary commitments to knowledge production beyond reductive forms of economic reason and control is just too risky for capital. The kinds of educational innovations that hold the potential to promote greater social intelligence and more creatively inclined subjects capable of meaningful democratic participation in the world raise distinct problems for the neoliberal project, especially in light of its all-too-evident recent failures. Broad investments in creativity and human and social development and cooperation contain the potential to not only raise and circulate basic questions about the legitimacy and sustainability of current economic, social, and political arrangements, but also inspire forms of intellectual and political engagement that contain the potential to challenge corporate–state power and enhance and expand human freedom and equality.

The subordination of creativity to neoliberal rationality highlights fundamental tensions concerning the value of knowledge and the democratic role of education. Rather than a social or public good necessary for promoting sustainable and democratic futures, knowledge is reduced to a private good valued primarily in terms of advancing narrow economic interests. Similarly, creativity is largely imagined as an economic capacity to be tamed and optimized through educational and corporate management rather than as a common oriented to social collaboration and democratization. The political task is thus to nurture those autonomous aspects of the common in educational spheres and society in order to build capacities toward subordinating political economy and technical knowledge to the common, as opposed to the other way around. It appears that education is increasingly at the center of struggles for what the future is going to look like—a future of broadly shared prosperity and sustainability, made possible through social cooperation and creativity, or one marked by continued scarcity, insecurity, and crisis for the majority.

Notes

1. See Michael A. Peters and Tina Besley. "Academic Entrepreneurship and the Creative Economy." *Thesis Eleven* 94 (2008): 88–105; Michael Peters, Simon Marginson, and Peter Murphy. *Creativity and the Global Knowledge Economy*. New York, NY: Peter Lang, 2008.
2. David Harvey. *The Enigma of Capital: And the Crises of Capitalism*. London, UK: Oxford University Press, 2010, 11.
3. Saskia Sassen. *Expulsions: Brutality and Complexity in the Global Economy*. Cambridge, MA: Belknap Press of Harvard University, 2014, 13.
4. Harvey, 2010.
5. Alain Touraine. *The Post-Industrial Society: Tomorrow's Social History: Classes, Conflicts and Culture in the Programmed Society*. Volume 6813. Random House, 1971; Daniel Bell. *The Coming of Post-Industrial Society*. New York, NY: Basic, 1973; Peter Drucker. *Post-Capitalist Society*. New York, NY: Routledge, 1994; Alvin Toffler. *The Third Wave*. New York, NY: Bantam Books, 1981; Nico Stehr. *Knowledge Societies*. London, UK: Sage, 1994; Robert Reich. *The Work of Nations: Preparing Ourselves for Twenty-First Century Capitalism*. New York, NY: Alfred Knopf, 1991; Manuel Castells. *The Information Age: Economy, Society and Culture: The Rise of the Network Society*. Volume 1. Malden, MA: Blackwell, 1996; Yochai Benkler. *The Wealth of Networks: How Social Production Transforms Markets and Freedom*. New Haven, CT: Yale University Press, 2006.

6   Nick Dyer-Witheford. *Cyber-Marx*. Urbana: University of Illinois Press, 1999.
7   Creative Industries Economic Estimates. January, 2015. Retrieved from https://www.gov.uk/government/publications/creative-industries-economic-estimates-january-2015/creative-industries-economic-estimates-january-2015-key-findings
8   John Howkins. *The Creative Economy: How People Make Money from Ideas*. New York, NY: Penguin. 2001; Richard Florida. *The Rise of the Creative Class: And How It's Transforming Work, Leisure, and Everyday Life*. New York, NY: Basic Books, 2003.
9   Florida, 2003, 21.
10 Ibid., 48.
11 Matteo Pasquinelli. "Immaterial Civil War, Prototypes of Conflict within Cognitive Capitalism." In Geert Lovink and Ned Rossiter (Eds.), *My Creativity Reader: Critique of Creative Industries*. Amsterdam: Institute of Network Cultures, 2007, 72–73.
12 For more on the history and elements of autonomist thought see Sylvère Lotringer and Christian Marazzi (Eds.). *Autonomia: Post-Political Politics*. Cambridge, MA: Semiotext(e), 2007.
13 Karl Marx. *Grundrisse*. New York, NY: Penguin, 1973.
14 Ibid., 706.
15 Carlo Vercellone. "From Formal Subsumption to General Intellect: Elements for a Marxist Reading of the Thesis of Cognitive Capitalism." *Historical Materialism* 15 (2007): 14.
16 Michael Hardt and Antonio Negri. *Commonwealth*. Cambridge, MA: Harvard University Press, 2009.
17 Ibid., 133.
18 Ibid., 132. Importantly, autonomist thinkers have been criticized for exaggerating the novelty and scope of biopolitical production. It is therefore best not to imagine cognitive capitalism as a radical break with patterns of accumulation centered on industrial production, but rather as an intensification of commodification of knowledge and the capture of value from social life and intellectual production, or what can simply be called the common. For a sharp critique see George Cafentzis and Silvia Federici. "Notes on the Edu-factory and Cognitive Capitalism." *EIPCP*, 2007. Retrieved from http://eipcp.net/transversal/0809/caffentzisfederici/en
19 Hardt and Negri, 2009, 12.
20 David Harvey. *The New Imperialism*. New York, NY: Verso, 2007.
21 See for instance, Paul Mason. *Postcapitalism: A Guide to Our Future*. New York, NY: Penguin, 2015; Jeremy Rifkin. *The Zero Marginal Cost Society*. New York, NY: Palgrave Macmillan, 2014.
22 Michael Hardt. "The Common in Communism." In Costas Douzinas and Slavoj Žižek (Eds.), *The Idea of Communism*. New York, NY: Verso, 2010: 136.
23 The EduFactory consists of radical academics, activists, and precarious university workers from across the world. Here I am drawing mainly on the Zero Issue of their journal. See EduFactory Collective. "The Double Crisis: Living on the Borders." *EduFactory Journal* Zero Issue (2010). Retrieved from www.edufactory.org
24 Thomas Friedman. "The New Untouchables." *New York Times*, October 20, 2009. Retrieved from www.nytimes.com/2009/10/21/opinion/21friedman.html
25 Ken Robinson. *Out of Our Minds: Learning to Be Creative*. West Sussex, UK: Capstone, 2001; Daniel Pink. *A Whole New Mind: Why Right-Brainers Will Rule the World*. New York, NY: Riverhead Books, 2005; Douglas Thomas and John Seely Brown. *A New Culture of Learning: Cultivating the Imagination for a World of Constant Change*. Create Space, 2011; Tony Wagner. *Creating Innovators: The Making of Young People Who Will Change the World*. New York, NY: Scribner, 2012.

26 21st Century Skills Framework. Retrieved from www.p21.org/our-work/p21-framework
27 A Nation at Risk. Retrieved from https://www2.ed.gov/pubs/NatAtRisk/risk.html
28 Michael Hardt. "US Education and the Crisis." *Uninomade*, 2010. Retrieved from www.uninomade.org/us-education-and-the-crisis/
29 For a thorough overview and critical analysis of these trends see Diane Ravitch. *Reign of Error*. New York, NY: Vintage, 2013.
30 Ibid.
31 See the report by the Alliance to Reclaim our Schools and the Center for Popular Democracy titled, "The Top of the Iceberg: Charter School Vulnerabilities to Waste Fraud and Abuse." Retrieved from https://populardemocracy.org/sites/default/files/Charter-Schools-National-Report_rev2.pdf
32 See Alan Singer. "Success Academy's War against Children." *Huffington Post*, February 2017. Retrieved from www.huffingtonpost.com/alan-singer/success-academys-war-agai_b_9235556.html. See also Diane Ravitch's blog for analysis of Success Academies including letters by former teachers outlining the culture: https://dianeravitch.net
33 For a sharp analysis and overview of the misguided nature of US education reform, scripted curriculum, testing, and the centrality of class inequality to educational outcomes, see David C. Berliner and Gene V. Glass. *50 Myths and Lies that Threaten America's Public Schools: The Real Crisis in Education*. New York, NY: Teachers College Press, 2014.
34 Paulo Freire. *Pedagogy of the Oppressed*. New York, NY: Bloomsbury, 2000.
35 Linda M. McNeil. *Contradictions of Control: School Structure and School Knowledge*. New York, NY: Routledge, 2013.
36 See Wayne Au. *Unequal by Design: High-Stakes Testing and the Standardization of Inequality*. Routledge, 2010; Mark Garrison. *A Measure of Failure: The Political Origins of Standardized Testing*. SUNY Press, 2009.
37 Lyndsey Layton. "Majority of US Public School Students Are in Poverty." *Washington Post*, January 15, 2016. Retrieved from https://www.washingtonpost.com/local/education/majority-of-us-public-school-students-are-in-poverty/2015/01/15/df7171d0-9ce9-11e4-a7ee-526210d665b4_story.html?utm_term=.c9927bfd3478
38 Sean F. Reardon. "The Widening Academic Achievement Gap between the Rich and the Poor: New Evidence and Possible Explanations." In Greg Duncan and Richard Murnane (Eds.), *Whither Opportunity?* Russell Sage, 2011: 91–116; Sean F. Reardon. "The Widening Income Achievement Gap." *Educational Leadership* 70, no. 8 (2013): 10–16.
39 David Berliner. "Effects of Inequality and Poverty vs. Teachers and Schooling on America's Youth." *Teachers College Record* 115, no. 12 (2013): 1–26.
40 Pat Garofalo. "How Illinois' Flawed Funding System Shortchanges Chicago's Students." ThinkProgress, September 12, 2012. Retrieved from https://thinkprogress.org/how-illinois-flawed-funding-system-shortchanges-chicago-s-students-c7628651d97c
41 Kenneth Saltman. "Comprehending Trump's Secretary of Education." *Breaking Out*. Retrieved from http://breakingout.net.au/content/comprehending-trumps-education-secretary; Joanne Barkan. "Milton Friedman, Betsy DeVos, and the Privatization of Public Education." *Dissent*, January 17, 2017. Retrieved from https://www.dissentmagazine.org/online_articles/betsy-devos-milton-friedman-public-education-privatization; Jason Blakely. "How School Choice Turns Education into a Commodity." *The Atlantic*, April 17, 2017.

42 Rotman Web, 2010. Retrieved from www.rotman.utoronto.ca/expansion/newbuilding.htm
43 Nick Dyer-Witheford. "Cognitive Capitalism and the Contested Campus." *European Journal of Higher Arts Education* 2 (2005): 71–93.
44 Marc Bousquet. *How the University Works: Higher Education and the Low Wage Nation.* New York, NY: NYU Press, 2008.
45 Christopher Newfield. "The Structure and Silence of the Cognotariat." *EduFactory Journal* Zero Issue (2010): 11.
46 Ibid., 11.
47 Ibid., 12.
48 Ibid., 11.
49 Christopher Newfield. *Unmaking the Public University: The Forty Year Assault on the Middle Class.* Cambridge, MA: Harvard University Press, 2008.
50 Mark Kantrowitz. "The Distribution of Grants and Scholarships by Race." Retrieved from www.finaid.org/scholarships/20110902racescholarships.pdf
51 Newfield, 2008, 6.
52 Wendy Brown. *Undoing the Demos: Neoliberalism's Stealth Revolution.* Brooklyn, NY: Zone Books, 2015, 180–181.
53 See Henry Giroux. "Higher Education and the Politics of Disruption." Truth Out, March 17, 2015. Retrieved from www.truth-out.org/news/item/29693-higher-education-and-the-politics-of-disruption
54 David Graeber. "Dead Zones of the Imagination: On Violence, Bureaucracy, and Interpretive Labor. The 2006 Malinowski Memorial Lecture." *HAU: Journal of Ethnographic Theory* 2, no. 2 (2012): 105–128.

5
DIGITIZATION: ALGORITHMIC LEARNING MACHINES

Popular narratives spun in 24/7 social media, through TED talks and Ideas Festivals, and in Silicon Valley public relations, suggest that emergent digital platforms based on the Internet of Things, predictive analytics, machine learning, and big data will produce a future of expanded efficiency, freedom, decentralization, openness, creativity, and cooperation. Driven by benevolent corporations and disruptive tech-entrepreneurship, it is argued that "digitization" will provide technical solutions to entrenched problems confronting societies. These solutionist ambitions have extended into K-12 schooling, where data processing and adaptive analytics are being promoted as a means of "customizing" and "personalizing" learning in the name of "reinventing" education for the twenty-first century.

Enthusiasm for new digital learning technology is understandable. It reflects a deeply rooted modern belief in capitalism and technology as drivers of social efficiency and progress. It also reflects current anxieties over the role and purpose of public schooling within changing historical circumstances marked by precarity and technological acceleration. What I refer to in this chapter as "algorithmic education" is presented as a new and innovative means to produce the human capital and cognitive and technical capacities required to boost GDP and create employment within a global "knowledge economy" and "information society."[1] Algorithmic education, it is argued, will deliver a dynamic multidimensional curriculum outside of the brick-and-mortar constraints of industrial schooling customized to each individual student. Moreover, advocates for algorithmic education suggest that if digital platforms such as Google, Netflix, Amazon, and Facebook have transformed the way we conduct business, work, shop, communicate, travel, debate, and entertain one another, then it only makes sense to apply the operational logics of these platforms to educational systems in the name of progress and innovation. "Technologies have amplified our desires for choice, flexibility and individualization," Phil McRae notes, "so it is easy to be seduced by a vision of computers delivering only what we want, when, and how we want it customized." This has produced an expectation that "a flexible education system" based on digital tools "will also be more efficient and (cost) effective."[2]

Digital technologies do have fascinating potential to address global problems, as well as how we might imagine and practice education in the future. However, technology is always embedded within ideological assumptions and can have both dystopian and utopian potentials. Therefore technology narratives and applications can never be taken at face value and require critical assessment. Richard Kahn and Douglas Kellner have argued that "more than ever, we need philosophical reflection on the ends and purposes of educational technology, and on what we are doing and trying to achieve with it in our educational practices and institutions."[3] This chapter reflects on the push to "disrupt" and "customize" education through new technology. It examines the values and assumptions underlying algorithmic education and its claims to revolutionize teaching and learning as a means to solve the social, educational, and economic problems of the twenty-first century.

Algorithmic Education

It has long been an ambition to create a perfect learning machine. One modern example is the teaching machine invented by Sidney Pressey in 1926. The machine was a simple box with a window and four buttons that skill-and-drilled students on scrolling punch-card multiple-choice questions. In the 1950s, B.F. Skinner applied his behaviorist psychology to develop another mechanical push-button learning machine based in stimulus and response theories of behavioral modification.[4] Since the 1970s and 1980s, a wide variety of computer-based learning programs have been used in schools. While there have been many prior predictions that computers would make schools and teachers irrelevant, as the education scholar Larry Cuban has noted, most of these efforts to integrate computer technology and software in schools have had very little effect on education or improving teaching and learning—as he put it, "computers meet classroom, classroom wins."[5]

The desire to create a perfect learning machine has not waned and is now being articulated in a new movement to "customize" and "revolutionize" education through digital platforms.[6] In light of decades of perceived failure, US schools have been declared bereft of creativity and innovation and therefore primed for entrepreneurial disruption through new technology. Silicon Valley firms such as Facebook and Amazon, venture philanthropies like the Gates and Walton family foundations, Wall Street banks such as Goldman Sachs and Citibank, and major media corporations such as News Corporation have been investing unprecedented venture capital into educational technology—$2.5 billion in the first half of 2015 alone—while championing the idea that big-data platforms, cloud computing, predictive analytic software, and cyber-charter schools can succeed where other market-driven reforms have failed, by offering technological solutions to longstanding structural problems in public education.[7] Mark Zuckerberg and Bill Gates have both thrown their financial resources behind digital learning technology after becoming disillusioned by the lackluster results of privatization and high-stakes testing embodied in the No Child Left Behind, Race to the Top, and Common Core initiatives.

As a set of practices, algorithmic education can be imagined as a mode of "digital Taylorism" that replays the dreams of school administrators from the early twentieth century such as David Snedden and Elwood Cubberley, who sought to apply the managerial logic and organizational structure of the factory in order to rationalize all aspects of public education based on the scientific management theories of Frederick Winslow Taylor.[8] However, departing from earlier efficiency movements, which were oriented firmly within a Fordist paradigm of state-managed capitalism and industrial administration, algorithmic education seeks to harness decentralized market forces, speculative logics, Silicon Valley innovation, and the network intelligence of the Internet of Things in order to "revolutionize" teaching and learning through digitization. The stated goal is to break down the older inefficient bureaucratic hierarchies and "one-size-fits-all" schemas in order to "reinvent" education for the twenty-first century. Enthusiasts thus suggest it represents a cutting-edge alternative to factory models of public schooling that are now, like the nominally social democratic Keynesian welfare state, considered irrelevant in an age of global "cognitive" capitalism.[9]

Digital technologies combined with entrepreneurial energies, it is argued, will enable a profound revolution in educational efficiency and quality. In the words of Jennifer Medbery, CEO of the edu-tech company Kickboard, tech entrepreneurs "see a disruptive opportunity to 'democratize' education" as new digital technologies "increase the efficiency of the learning market by lowering barriers to knowledge acquisition."[10] This entrepreneur-led revolution is to be achieved through integrative algorithmic learning platforms that will link together all aspects of a student's life activity within and beyond schools. Former Republican congressman Newt Gingrich, a well-known dabbler in popular tech futurism and zealous corporate school reform advocate, pontificates:

> Get schools out of the 1890s ... In an age when most information and knowledge is transmitted digitally and is increasingly personalized—think about how Netflix, Pandora, Twitter and Facebook work—we should be able to do much better than that. Pioneering projects like Khan Academy, Udacity and Coursera are pointing toward a future of learning that is more like Netflix than the chalk-and-textbook system we have today.[11]

At this point, in order to illustrate how algorithmic education actually functions in practice, I want to turn to an example of a personal adaptive learning system from a United States Department of Education report titled *Enhancing Teaching and Learning through Educational Data Mining and Learning Analytics* (2012) (see Figure 5.1).[12]

DIGITIZATION 101

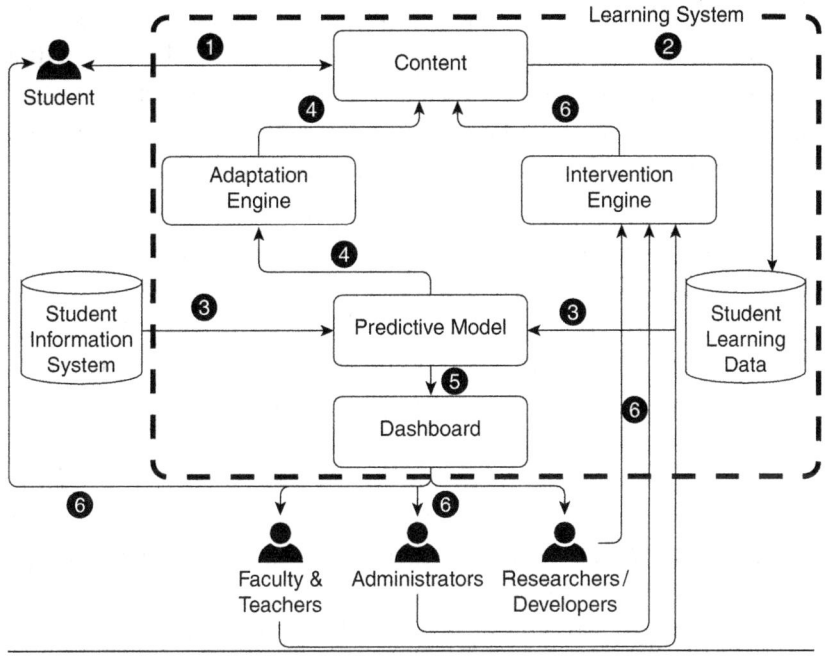

Figure 5.1 Components of a Typical Adaptive Learning System

Let us take a brief journey in order to understand this adaptive learning model. This requires following along the numbered arrows in the chart. To begin at arrow one, the student is connected to learning "content" through some form of digital screen interface, such as a tablet or laptop. Second, "student learning data" is then produced as the student performs a series of tasks by interacting with the learning "content" such as answering a battery of standardized test questions. Third, this "student learning data" is simultaneously transmitted to a "student information system" database and also into "a predictive model." Fourth, the "predictive model" deploys algorithms through an "adaptive engine," which in turn creates new personalized student-learning "content" in an endless feedback loop. Fifth, the data points produced through adaptive student learning are registered on a dashboard for teachers, administrators, and developers so that they may analyze and assess student learning and the "efficacy" of the learning system.

Algorithmic education is based on the production of data generated through student interaction with digital screen interfaces that is then subjected to predictive algorithms as the central expertise guiding teaching and learning. In turn, this process redefines the role of the teacher as a data analyst and the student as a monadic actor engaged in a circular process of digital interaction and data generation. The data produced through these interactions can then be stored and mined for a variety of purposes, such as making judgments on future educational and economic pathways for students, and/or potentially sold as a commodity to third parties. This model of adaptive learning thus mirrors consumer platforms such as Netflix, Google, Amazon, Pandora, Facebook, and iTunes. Through our interaction with these digital platforms, billions of data points are produced that are then routed through algorithms in order to track our behaviors and preferences, create personalized advertising and future products in an endless feedback loop. Within algorithmic education, it is specifically *schools and students* that become the *producers, consumers, and products* as they interact with adaptive systems, which are the intellectual property of corporations, thus blurring the lines between public schools and the private domain of technology companies and their software developers.

For instance, Jose Ferreira, the founder and CEO of Knewton Inc, an adaptive learning company backed by Silicon Valley powerhouses such as PayPal founder and Trump supporter Peter Thiel and partnered with corporate behemoths such as Pearson, has compared algorithmic education to having "a friendly robot tutor in the sky that can semi-read your mind and figure out what your strengths and weaknesses are, down to the percentile."[13] He observes: "Knewton plucks perfect bits of content for you from the cloud and assembles them according to the ideal learning strategy for you, as determined by the combined data-power of millions of other students." Ferreira continues: "we literally know everything about what you know, how you learn best, everything … We have five orders of magnitude more data about you than Google has … We literally have more data about our students than any company has about anybody else about anything, and it's not even close."[14] Knewton's approach is indicative of a broader sociotechnical imaginary animating the new algorithmic education movement, based on an instrumental view of education where machines are positioned as the key to unlocking human potentiality.

What is perhaps most immediately striking about the model of algorithmic education outlined in the diagram above is that it dramatically attenuates human relationships and social interaction within the process of teaching and learning. The underlying assumption appears to be that the replacement of dialogue and social cooperation through predictive software is both desirable and effective as a means of producing meaningful educational experiences. Personalization, flexibility, adaptability, decentralization, creativity, and innovation are all thought to flow naturally from a student–screen–data–algorithm matrix. In this sense, algorithmic education reflects a techno-determinist ethos consisting of distinct sociotechnical rationalities that frame complex social processes as *computational problems* to be solved through "smart systems" powered by data processing, cloud computing, and machine learning.[15] This imagines technology as a neutral and objective force of progress beyond ideology or politics. For instance, problems such as racial segregation and social inequality are simply framed as "design problems" to be fixed through educational apps and learning software, as opposed to historical and structural issues requiring distinct sociopolitical responses.[16]

Algorithmic education can thus be framed within various critical intellectual traditions that have examined modern forms of technocratic rationalization immanent to capitalism, science, state institutions, and mass psychology. For instance, foundational critics of modernity such as Max Weber and those associated with the Frankfurt School have observed how modern instrumental rationalities such as those embodied by algorithmic learning systems can serve to naturalize and perpetuate the domination of human beings and the natural world through the conflation of quantification, calculation, measurement, efficiency, and technical mastery with progress.[17] This reflects a "colonization of the lifeworld by systems," in the language of Jürgen Habermas, and/or an instantiation of Herbert Marcuse's "totally administered society," where technocratic rationality "transforms the object world into an extension of man's mind and body ... they find their soul in their automobile, hi-fi set, split-level home, kitchen equipment."[18] Pushing these ideas further, feminist thinkers such as Donna Haraway, Sandra Harding, Chandra Mohanty, and Vandana Shiva have argued that instrumental rationality is one component in a broader arc of modern development that cannot be understood outside of how capitalism, science, and technology have been intricately woven into histories and experiences of Eurocentrism, patriarchy, racism, colonialism, imperialism, and ecological degradation.[19]

Such observations sync with various strands of progressive and critical educational philosophy that have identified how technocratic rationalities applied to educational institutions and contexts have often been implicated in the erosion of creativity, cooperation, dialogue, agency, imagination, and engaged inquiry. However, as Richard Kahn and Douglas Kellner point out in their insightful analysis, key progressive and radical educational thinkers such as John Dewey, Maxine Greene, Paulo Freire, and Ivan Illich, although oriented differently in their respective intellectual projects, each understood that it is not enough to critique the instrumental and/or oppressive applications of technology in education. Rather, technology must also be critically assessed in relation to its potential to both *limit and enhance* human freedom and knowledge, and contribute to future projects of social transformation and educational reconstruction. "Against one-sided critiques of present educational technology that are overly technophilic or technophobic," Kahn and Kellner view technology as "complex and contested by a variety of forces, rich with alternatives that are immediately present yet ideologically, normatively, or otherwise blocked from achieving their full realization."[20]

In this spirit, it must be noted that science, expertise, engineering, programming, code, design, economic production and exchange, and emergent technologies are all crucial elements in realizing futures beyond the limits of neoliberal society. At issue are the systems of value, power, and rationality in which these fields are embedded. As Donna Haraway notes, "technology is not neutral. We're inside of what we make, and it's inside of us. We're living in a world of connections—and it matters which ones get made and unmade."[21] With this in mind, we might begin to think through and imagine how algorithmic education could become a tool for progressive and emancipatory possibilities for education and society. However, this requires avoiding the seduction of technophobia as well as techno-determinism by attending to the contradictions, ideological assumptions, and empirical limitations of the new sociotechnical educational imaginary.

Optimizing Digital Futures

Algorithmic education reflects a web of corporate interests and speculative narratives that project sociotechnical solutions and futures for schools and society based on digital technology platforms. The educational scholar Ben Williamson uses the terminology of "sociotechnical imaginary" and "algorithmic imaginary" to describe the assumptions and values animating the new corporate-driven algorithmic educational technology movement. *Sociotechnical imaginaries* refer to modes of dominant thinking concerning desired visions of social life and the future that are widely held, embedded in institutions and practices, and underwritten by technology narratives and innovations. These are not "just science fiction fantasies," Williamson writes; "the dreamscapes of the future that are dreamt up in science laboratories and technical R&D departments ... are used in the design of actual technologies and scientific innovations" that then "materialize the desired future."[22] In this sense, sociotechnical imaginaries are cognitive maps, models, blueprints, and diagrams through which attempts are made by certain actors to make reality conform.

While sociotechnical imaginaries reflect the construction of technology futures, *algorithmic imaginaries* are specific to the forms of rationality and value emerging from Silicon Valley and its solutionist culture. Algorithmic imaginaries reflect calculative rationalities that seek to optimize various aspects of social life and human interaction by subjecting reality to technical expertise and systems regulation in an attempt to make it measurable and knowable through the production of data. Data, in turn, enables human action and interaction to become subject to prediction, intervention, optimization, and "enhancement" as it is routed through predictive algorithms that anticipate and shape future behaviors and actions. As Google CEO Eric Schmidt once quipped, "I actually think most people don't want Google to answer their questions, they want Google to tell them what they should be doing next."[23] Such logic assumes that the complexities of social life, human psychology, value, desire, communication, and cognition can be reduced to "data points," or measurable and optimizable units. As Williamson states:

> The notion of an algorithmic imaginary ... captures the Silicon Valley ideal of calculating, predicting and pre-empting human behaviors and social institutions through technical platforms that are increasingly automated and data-driven. The technocratic ideal of complete scientific calculability and technical objectivity associated with algorithmic practice underpins its approach.[24]

The sociotechnical and algorithmic imaginary driving the edu-tech revolution is constructing new futures of public schooling underwritten by corporate and Silicon Valley mindsets and sociotechnical visions regarding the future of education as a set of customizable actions and metrics to be commercialized, quantified, and optimized. An important subtext, of course, is that educational optimization through algorithmic learning is framed as a superior means to boost human capital to serve the economic imperatives of the twenty-first century. I want to turn here to an extended example of these logics.

A Glimpse into the Future

Knowledge Works is a self-described "philanthropy," "operating foundation," and "social enterprise" with a presence in more than 30 US states, and a major booster of algorithmic learning. Knowledge Works specializes in what it calls "strategic forecasting," a speculative practice that seeks to model and project technology futures for education and society. The future of education imagined by Knowledge Works is one that is radically customized through technology and mediated by commercial interests. This is education "unbundled" from traditional schools and redistributed in personalized learning "grids" and "ecosystems" created by edu-preneurs and unfettered market forces.

In their strategic forecast, "Recombinant Education: Regenerating the Learning Ecosystem," Knowledge Works identifies key "disruptions" that are set to reshape education in the next decades.[25] First, in what they call "democratized startup," Knowledge Works envisions a "new open social and financial infrastructure," which will decentralize entrepreneurship. "Open access to startup knowledge, expertise, and networks will seed an explosion of disruptive social innovations," they assert, creating "transformational networks of collective economic and social impact" turning "any teacher, parent, or student into an edu-preneur." These armies of "edu-preneurs will stimulate continuous learner-centered recombinations across the learning ecosystem."

Second, in what they call "high fidelity living," Knowledge Works predicts that "as big data floods human sensemaking capacities, cognitive assistants and contextual feedback systems" will be developed by disruptive edu-preneurs that will shore up "our minds with software assistants" and help us "discern information flows." New developments in understanding of cognition and motivation will also improve our "understanding of how to structure learning and work environments to maximize focus, intrinsic motivation, and creativity." Data analytics will help "learning agents [teachers] provide preemptive" and "whole-person support based on factors such as learners' [students] health, environments, and social contexts, and their academic performance."

Third, in what they refer to as "de-institutionalized production," Knowledge Works predicts a shift from a "workforce to a talent cloud" with "organizations relying on global networks of independent talent to match specialized skills with interaction-based tasks." Think here of an intensification of just-in-time "gig" labor provided by platforms such as Uber and TaskRabbit. This will occur simultaneously with an intensification of automation that will replace workers with robots, "giving rise to steel-collared workers." Knowledge Works predicts that "extreme career mobility will become the norm" and "career readiness will be a continuous and dynamic need over a lifetime, requiring self-directed learning that is closely aligned to the needs of social production networks."

Fourth, Knowledge Works envisions "customizable value webs," consisting of "innovative, open business models" that "will leverage complex networks of assets and relationships to create ultra-customer-centric experiences." New digital platforms, edu-tech start-ups, and social enterprises will reimagine schools as rich "customer-centric" ecosystems of learning opportunities distributed across space and time. "Customer-centric value propositions will guide the creation of learning experiences" as well as "rich value webs to serve distinct populations ... recombining experiences, assets, and tools to help each learner find the specific value propositions that best meet his or her needs."

The sociotechnical imaginary of Knowledge Works views disruptive innovation and commercialization of education as inevitable and progressive. Entrepreneurs and technology companies, within this view, always and only have altruistic intentions of making "social impact" and contributing to "social production" within new networks of "edu-preneurship," "conscious investment," "sharing economies," and "rich value-webs." Moreover, digital technologies are viewed as a means to customize education through the development of new data networks and infrastructures. Students and families will create their own "learning playlists" of "learning content" that are radically personalized through digital tools and platforms and endless streams of data. Rather than making students listen to the same lectures and do the same activities, every student will have his/her own learning map, "customized" according to learner profiles at every level, just as platforms like Netflix and Amazon customize products based on customer profiles. Knowledge Works predicts that as employment becomes more precarious, flexible, short-term, task-oriented, elusive, and subject to automation and robotics, human capital for the labor market will shift to forms of learning unbundled from traditional brick-and-mortar schools. The view is that, in a highly fragmented labor market marked by extreme flexibility, education should also be deconstructed and redistributed across a network of organizations and new service providers that offer branded "customer-centric" learning opportunities that are all linked together via networked smart systems, data processing, mobile apps, and software.

Within the sociotechnical and algorithmic imaginary of Knowledge Works, teaching is therefore conceptualized as a mobile and deliverable technology service, and learning as a product made possible by "open business models," "edu-preneurs," and a host of other "social enterprises."Teachers are defined as "learning agents," "coaches," and "guides" who monitor students through flows of learning tasks, learning data, and learning outcomes driven by algorithms. Teachers no longer teach, but facilitate the algorithm-as-teaching machine. Students are reconfigured as "learners" subject to perpetual assessment and optimization.

Ultimately, decentralized digital learning ecosystems are presented as the means to produce the dynamic human-capital abilities required to serve markets and solve the problems of the twenty-first century.

Transcendence and Antagonism

The vision of educational futures offered by Knowledge Works is one of personal "empowerment," "social impact," "creativity," and "liberation" from current educational limitations, all through the advancement of "disruptive" edu-tech entrepreneurship emerging spontaneously from market signals, investments, and exchanges. This sociotechnical imaginary tracks with a deeply held belief in the utopian potential of capitalism and technology. Within this frame, markets and digitization are positioned as a means to transcend the limits imposed by contemporary social arrangements (such as public schools), and even capitalism itself. Such views are far from unique today. In his recent book *The Zero Marginal Cost Society*, Jeremy Rifkin suggests that digitization and the Internet of Things are inexorably leading to the transformation of global society, whereby an emerging collaborative commons will displace capitalism altogether.[26] Rifkin observes:

> The Internet of Things will connect everything with everyone in an integrated global network. People, machines, natural resources, production lines, logistics networks, consumption habits, recycling flows, and virtually every other aspect of economic and social life will be linked via sensors to the IoT platform, continually feeding Big Data to every node—businesses, homes, vehicles—moment to moment in real time. Big Data in turn will be processed with advanced analytics, transformed into predictive algorithms, and programmed into automated systems to improve thermodynamic efficiencies and dramatically increase productivity, and reduce the range and cost of producing and delivering a range of goods and services at near zero cost across the entire economy.[27]

According to Rifkin, the IoT, combined with new DIY maker cultures, open-access software, peer-to-peer networks, digital currencies such as

Bitcoin, social-media platforms, 3D printing, crowdsourcing, and other digital innovations are slowly beginning to undermine capitalist profit models and intellectual property. He observes:

> Hundreds of millions of people are already transferring bits and pieces of their economic life from capitalist markets to the global Collaborative Commons. Prosumers are not only sharing and producing their own information, entertainment, green energy, 3D-printed goods, and massive open online courses on the Collaborative Commons at near zero marginal cost. They are also sharing cars, homes, and even clothes with one another via social media sites, rentals, redistribution clubs, and cooperatives, at low or near zero marginal cost.[28]

Echoing Knowledge Works, Rifkin argues that a new brand of "social entrepreneurship" is emerging wherein "social capital" is becoming more important than financial capital, concerns over sustainability are replacing consumerism, cooperation is replacing competition, and social value is replacing exchange value. According to Rifkin, this is engendering a transition from a capitalist model based on private property and private accumulation of profit, to one of sharing and collective benefit rooted in a dynamic, digitally networked, collaborative commons. Rifkin observes that this is creating a radical revaluation of how to measure economic performance, with concerns over GDP replaced by social priorities such as "quality of life" indices and other measures of human wellbeing and ecological sustainability. Taking all this together, Rifkin argues that by midcentury the collaborative commons will eclipse both capitalism and the bureaucratic state as the dominant organizing frame for human existence and global civil society.

The problem with Rifkin's analysis, along with other similar expressions of techno-transcendence such as that of Knowledge Works, is not that the future he describes is necessarily undesirable, or that digitization and the IoT do not pose interesting possibilities for constructing new modes of economic and social production and exchange, but that it completely ignores questions of power and antagonism. For Rifkin, the technological and innovative features of capitalism embodied by digitization are leading to the inexorable transcendence of capitalism and its institutional foundations in private property, commodification of labor, and a systemic drive to perpetual growth and accumulation. However, while IoT-based platforms and algorithmic technologies may amplify certain non-capitalist aspects of the commons, this does not mean an inevitable progressive or transcendent trajectory. On the contrary, rather than creating a friction-free global commons based on sharing and the triumph of social value over exchange value, as Rifkin suggests, new digital technologies, in so far as they are squarely integrated into the power dynamics of global capitalism and the endless commodification of nature and society, can just as readily be viewed as enhancing exploitation, hierarchy, and imperialism.

New technologies such as open-access software, social-media platforms, big data, network infrastructures, cloud computing, predictive analytics, and artificial intelligence occupy a central node within this broader terrain of conflict. On the one hand, as Rifkin suggests, these technologies are indeed generating possibilities for new forms of collaboration, value, creativity, labor, and social capacity that call into question dominant economic and political arrangements. Sharing platforms, digital currencies, P2P networks, commons licensing, 3D printing, machine learning, and big data do present interesting challenges to profit models based on maintaining the scarcity of knowledge and private monopoly over intellectual property. Moreover, Twitter, Facebook, YouTube, and other social-media platforms have played a crucial role in politics and in oppositional movements in recent years, from Chile to Iran, Quebec, Tunisia, Spain, New York, and Hong Kong. The Women's March against the Trump administration in January 2017 organized on Facebook brought an astounding ten million people into the streets globally. At the same time, technology is implicated in new articulations of irrationality, illiteracy, narcissism, surveillance, and social control. Corporate and state entities such as Google, Amazon, Facebook, and the NSA are aggressively erecting systems to mobilize and contain social media and data technologies for the purpose of creating monopolies and enhancing private accumulation and social control. Likewise, sharing platforms such as Uber and TaskRabbit, rather than "liberating" and "empowering" individuals to become the CEOs of their own micro-enterprises, are reshaping the terms of worker exploitation and intensifying the precaritization of work. As Steven Hill notes, "companies like Upwork, TaskRabbit and Freelancer.com have created 'labor brokerage' websites and mobile apps, many of which amount to online auctions in which vulnerable workers bid against each other for work, driving down wages to that of the lowest bidder."[29] Moreover, algorithms and data platforms are far from neutral. As Harvard-trained mathematician and former Wall Street risk manager Cathy O'Neil has documented in her book *Weapons of Math Destruction*, big data and algorithms are based on practices of profiling and surveillance designed to benefit the interests of those who own the tools.[30]

> Big data essentially is a way of separating winners and losers. Big data profiles people. It has all sorts of information about them—consumer behavior, everything available in public records, voting, demography. It profiles people and then it sorts people into winners and losers ... Are you persuadable as a voter or are you not persuadable as a voter? Are you likely to be vulnerable to a payday loan advertisement or are you impervious to that payday loan advertisement? So you have scores in a multitude of ways. The framing of it by the people who own these models is that it's going to benefit the world because more information is better. When, of course, what's really going on ... is that it's a rigged system, a system based on surveillance and on asymmetry of information.[31]

What we can observe is a struggle over the application and effects of algorithmic and data technologies that internalizes a multiplicity of conflicts over values, transparency, power, and decision-making. Whose values are being reflected? Whose interests are being served? Who owns and benefits from these technologies? What are the implications for privacy, ethics, agency, and democracy? Data technologies are capable of tracking and linking together an individual's search and browser history, driving records, health records, educational records, media and consumption habits, moral and political sensibilities, and eating and exercise habits. Such information is a highly lucrative commodity bought and sold by corporations on the open market and can be used to determine insurance premiums, screen applicants for employment, make predictions on criminal behavior, and/or approve or deny loans, all without our knowledge or consent.[32]

The rhetoric of social impact, customization, creativity, and social enterprise animating current sociotechnical and algorithmic imaginaries serves to obscure the structural conditions and economic interests and power relations shaping the "smartification" and "datafication" of life and their potential impact on human interaction and social outcomes.[33] For example, if there are higher rates of crime in poor, racially isolated urban neighborhoods, then predictive crime-fighting algorithms will direct police to those neighborhoods, where black and brown youth, who use and distribute illegal drugs at comparable rates to their white counterparts, will be subject to profiling, thus reproducing the racial logic of mass incarceration and feeding into the US market in private prisons. Something like a pre-crime division imagined in the Philip K. Dick short story "Minority Report" becomes a tangible possibility as criminal justice is increasingly "optimized." This speaks to what technology writer Evgeny Morozov refers to as "algorithmic regulation," governing society as a series of *surface effects* to be managed by feedback loops, sensors, apps, and data processing as opposed to *deeply rooted causal processes* that require ethical reflection and political action. Morozov writes: "as Silicon Valley keeps corrupting our language with its endless glorification of disruption and efficiency—concepts at odds with the vocabulary of democracy—our ability to question the "how" of politics is weakened."[34] Such conflicts over the *digital commons* are immanent to the aims of corporations and Silicon Valley to pursue profit no matter how altruistic or utopian the language that is used. These tensions should disabuse us of techno-utopian fantasies of friction-free transcendence of capitalism. At the same time, we have a critical perspective from which to return our analysis of algorithmic education.

Algorithmic Education as a Neoliberal Conflict Machine

Algorithmic education is frequently described with altruistic language of social impact and empowerment. Technology will enable a profound revolution in schooling by personalizing learning so that all young people have the capacities and skills they need to succeed, thereby producing better livelihoods and a better society. However, what must be understood first and foremost is that algorithmic education is big business. In the United States, major Silicon Valley firms such as Facebook, Wall Street banks such as Goldman Sachs, and venture philanthropies such as the Gates (Microsoft) and Walton (Walmart) foundations are currently committing billions to support educational technology start-ups.[35] Major technology and media companies including Microsoft, Apple, Google, and News Corp are also aggressively marketing tablet hardware and learning software to school districts. This represents a highly coordinated effort to capture profit from educational systems.

The global educational marketplace stands at approximately $5 trillion a year. The potential for gargantuan profit in education rivals the health and insurance markets. The market for "e-learning" products in higher education, such as digital tools for MOOCs (massive open online courses), is $91 billion alone. In 2011/2012, sales to US elementary and high schools for software and digital content neared $8 billion dollars. There was an astonishing $2.5 billion invested in edu-tech companies in the first half of 2015, shattering prior records.[36] As Neil Selwyn notes, "the shaping of digital education around the pursuit of profit is stronger than ever before."[37] Corporations extract value by gaming public policies such as Race to the Top and Common Core to generate profit through charter school management and real-estate deals, as well as contracts for IT infrastructures and technology services. For instance, corporations such as Pearson and McGraw-Hill capture rent-based profit as school districts pay millions to access online materials, analytic software, databases and cloud storage, and digital curriculum and testing platforms through subscription fees that can require an endless cycle of billing.[38] Teacher and student data produced through digital learning environments and software systems also represents a potential lucrative source of *capitalist rent*, where access to school databases can be sold to generate targeted advertising and drive decision-making in relation to new product development and even future hiring decisions. Digital storage and commodification of student data thus gives new weight to the idea of a "permanent record" as big data is poised to follow students through the life course. Further, the bundling of public investments and private loans for charter school deals and outlays for educational technology into stocks, securities, and derivative instruments represents a source of speculative profit for Wall Street banks, hedge funds, and rich private investors.

Algorithmic technology enthusiasts deny being motivated by profit. Instead they suggest that adaptive systems can be used to personalize and customize teaching and learning in order to efficiently develop and enhance the cognitive and non-cognitive capacities of each individual student and thereby radically improve education. Adaptive learning developers are selectively drawing on research in neuroscience, psychology, sociology, and child development in order to construct algorithmic learning regimes that can promote, assess, and capture data points not only on cognitive abilities (rendered narrowly as "skills"), but also on affective dispositions such as perseverance, resiliency, tenacity, creativity—even "thinking" itself. In an especially visceral example, an online tutoring system called Wayang Outpost uses four biometric sensor systems on students to measure and collect data on affective dispositions and engagement such as levels of frustration, motivation, confidence, boredom, and fatigue. First, the *mood meter* sensor purports to measure emotions. It uses a camera to capture students' facial expressions and software to measure the distance between the corners of the students' lips and their eyes in order to provide a *smile intensity score* that supposedly measures "engagement." Second, a sensor called the *posture analysis seat* is used to detect boredom and fatigue by measuring student movements such as fidgeting and twitching. Third, a hand-held *pressure mouse* is used to measure levels of frustration. Fourth, a *wireless skin conductance sensor* is used to assess levels of stress in students. For each student, researchers combined the data from these sensors and feedback systems and used machine-learning techniques to determine how sensor data and online learning behaviors relate to student attitudes toward math.[39]

All of this smacks of pure, uncut quackery. Nonetheless, it is confidently asserted that such algorithmic learning systems will contribute to developing the human capital, creative capacities, and gritty self-determination necessary to stimulate economic growth and solve twenty-first-century problems. There is, however, no actual evidence to support these claims. Quite the contrary—a global study conducted by the OECD and published in 2015 found that frequent use of computers in schools is actually more likely to be associated with lower levels of learning and lower educational outcomes. The report compared more than 70 countries on the international PISA examination and found that students who use computers frequently at school demonstrate lower levels of learning, and that there are "no appreciable improvements" in reading, mathematics or science in countries that have invested heavily in learning technology.[40] Commenting on the findings, the director of the OECD education division Andreas Schleicher states: "if you look at the best-performing education systems, such as those in East Asia, they've been very cautious about using technology in their classrooms ... those students who use tablets and computers very often tend to do worse than those who use them moderately." He further notes that in relation to equity, "one of the most disappointing findings of the report is that the socio-economic divide between students is not narrowed by technology, perhaps even amplified."[41]

While there is zero scientific evidence that adaptive learning systems and online learning are superior to professional educators and dynamic classrooms based on critical inquiry, dialogue, equity, philosophies of holistic child development, and socially engaged learning, there is a growing body of research that suggests exposure to screen technologies can be quite harmful to the cognitive, physical, and affective development of children. The American Academy of Pediatrics and the Canadian Society of Pediatrics have each indicated that intensive exposure to TV, video games, tablets, smart phones, and laptops is associated with childhood cognitive impairment, learning disabilities, obesity, mental illness, aggression, and sleep deprivation.[42] Writing in *Psychology Today*, child psychiatrist Victoria Dunkley observes:

> children's brains are much more sensitive to electronics use than most of us realize. In fact, it doesn't take much electronic stimulation to throw a sensitive and still developing brain off track ... screen time disrupts sleep and desynchronizes the body clock ... desensitizes the brain's reward system ... overloads the sensory system, fractures attention.

Researchers studying the effects of excessive screen time on children compare the impact to a psychiatric condition called "digital dementia."[43]

While algorithmic education may provide new opportunities to profit from schools, students, and teachers, as a dominant approach to education it appears unlikely to produce either high-skilled workers with dynamic human capital and/or healthy and flourishing human beings and communities. Despite the euphoric promises of personalization and empowerment, in its dominant conceptualization (see Figure 5.1 above), algorithmic learning is anti-relational, anti-dialogical, and rooted in assumptions of education and child development that do not accord with social and cognitive science. This contradiction has to be understood in relation to a precarious neoliberal debt-and-austerity economy marked by growing class stratification, state-budget crises, erosion of secure employment, and the desire of corporations to find new arenas of profit. Corporate school reform advocates and technology entrepreneurs openly discuss how algorithmic education will contribute to cutting costs, dismantle teacher unions, deskill professional teacher labor, and reduce the need for highly trained and certified professional educators.

For example, in their book *Liberating Learning*, John Chubb and Terry Moe, longstanding supporters of the privatization and corporatization of public schools, argue that technology is inevitably leading to the obsolescence of public schools. This is a good thing, they argue, because "government" schools (i.e. public schools) are necessarily inefficient, and markets and technology are necessarily efficient. Cyberschools and adaptive software will dramatically improve education by making teachers less necessary. They write that "fewer teachers will be necessary as students receive more instruction electronically" and this will mean that "schools become more efficient—changing the mix of teachers and technology and getting more bang (learning) for the buck."[44] For Chubb and Moe, teachers are considered a primary drag on productivity, efficiency, and cost. They are also barriers to improvement as they make what are considered unreasonable demands such as living wages, small class sizes, and the independence to make professional judgments on curriculum, pedagogy, and assessment.

The Canadian educational scholar Phil McRae notes that adaptive and online learning models have been "shown to reduce the teaching force to a 1 to 150 pupil teacher ratio with the monitoring of students in computer labs, tutoring and marking supported by non-certificated staff with titles like 'Coaches', 'Facilitators' or 'Individual Learning Specialists'." Cyber-charter school providers such as K12 Inc., which is the largest for-profit online school provider in the United States, has a student-to-teacher ratio of 275:1 and pays teachers far below their public-school counterparts: an average of $35,000 a year.[45] While cyber-charters generate profit for owners and investors by cutting labor costs and skimming public tax dollars, studies have consistently shown that they have been plagued by horrendous results and lack of oversight. Linda Darling-Hammond observes:

> scandals abound, especially with online charters, which have consistently negative outcomes yet reap the highest profits, since operators don't have to buy buildings and often hire few teachers at low salaries ... *The Columbus Dispatch* reported on the cyber-school ECOT in Ohio, which in one month received $932,030 in taxpayer money for 2,270 students, but could provide evidence that only seven had logged on.[46]

It is difficult to imagine elite parents and communities tolerating schools with a student-to-teacher ratio of 150:1 and/or schools that excessively employ reductive algorithmic learning regimes. It is well known that Silicon Valley executives such as the late Apple CEO Steve Jobs are often ruthless in limiting the screen time of their own children. Research on child development concludes unequivocally that children learn best and develop higher-order creativity and analytic ability through interaction with their caregivers, teachers, peers, environment, and books rather than from flickering pixels on a screen. This is precisely why Waldorf schools—expensive private schools with small student-to-teacher ratios where technology is completely absent from the learning environment—have become popular among Silicon Valley parents. Adam Alter notes:

> There's a school in Silicon Valley that doesn't allow the use of any tech. It's called the Waldorf School and it's fascinating because the school has no computers, no iPads, no iPhones. They try to minimize tech altogether and so people enjoy a lot of time face-to-face, they go outside a lot. What's interesting about this school is 75% of the students there are the children of Silicon Valley tech execs … These are people who, publicly, will expound on the wonders of the products they're producing and at the same time they decided in all their wisdom that their kids didn't belong in a school that used that same tech.[47]

A basic truth emerges here. The aim of "disrupting" and "optimizing" education through digitization is directed primarily at declining middle- and working-class communities far removed from the bubbles of elite privilege found in places like Silicon Valley. Moreover, algorithmic education does nothing to address or resolve the inequalities defining neoliberal political economy and that shape educational outcomes for young people. Instead, algorithmic learning technologies offer technocratic solutions and prescriptions for education based in corporate and Silicon Valley fantasies of technological mastery and optimization through commercial gadgetry. The realities of child poverty, evaporation of living wage employment, and intensifying economic and racial segregation shaping social reality can supposedly be overcome by optimizing schooling as a predictive data platform. These fantasies of mastery and technological transcendence are rooted in reductive notions of teaching and learning as quantification and technological transmission of information. This screens out deeper forms of cognitive, social, and emotional engagement with the world and others. Such a theory of schooling as a screen–data–algorithm matrix does not appear poised to produce more dynamic, empathic, creative, and entrepreneurial subjectivities inscribed in corporate educational reform rhetoric. The reality that many Silicon Valley parents reject such a model of schooling, teaching, and learning for their children should come as no surprise.

Beyond the Control Society

In a stagnant global capitalism with a general surplus of low- and high-skilled workers, technology represents a cost-effective and profitable way to educate youth whose future labor is increasingly expendable, from the standpoint of the precarious "gig" economy in which "extreme career flexibility" and unstable work are becoming the norm. On a deeper critical level, algorithmic education can be read as a tool to profit from and manage potential instabilities emanating from these precarious structural conditions. It not only embodies synergies with the security state where everyone is under surveillance at all times, but is also a powerful educational and cultural apparatus to standardize and contain teaching and learning as a prescriptive endeavor to serve markets and human capital, as opposed to a deeply humanistic affair aimed at producing mass intellectuality and democratic solidarities. Algorithmic education can thus be viewed as reorienting the reproductive features of schooling within what Gilles Deleuze evocatively refers to as the "society of control." This is a society in which surveillance and control become diffuse and all-encompassing as capital and state power are (1) *redistributed* through the organizational logic of the digital network, and (2) *recentralized* through the authority of the corporation. As Deleuze observes, "just as the corporation replaces the factory, *perpetual training* tends to replace the *school*, and continuous control to replace the examination. Which is the surest way of delivering the school over to the corporation."[48]

There is more than a grain of truth in the analogy of the control society. However, it is also incomplete, particularly as it doesn't take human agency into consideration. Algorithmic education is a fiercely contested issue within US education. Administrators, teachers, parents, and students are beginning to openly express opposition to the reductive use and commercial nature of algorithmic learning technology. One particularly high-profile case involved the data platform inBloom. Funded by the Gates and Carnegie foundations with $100 million in seed money, inBloom was to be the cornerstone of a "shared learning collaborative" described by a Gates spokesperson as an "amazing" software platform similar to a "huge app store ... with the Netflix and Facebook capabilities we love the most." The platform was designed to collect more than 400 data points that included personally identifiable student and teacher information. This information was to be explicitly shared with for-profit vendors without parental notification or consent. For instance, the data generated by inBloom was to be stored on a cloud serviced by Amazon with an operating system contracted to Amplify, a for-profit subsidiary of Rupert Murdoch's News Corporation. Between 2011 and 2014, nine US states had entered into partnerships with inBloom. However, concerns over privacy and commodification of student data began to circulate among parent groups and grass-roots organizations. Pushed by a campaign of opposition, states began to sever their ties with the company. In 2014, 40 Superintendents across the state of New York gave back federal Race to the Top funds in order to opt out of inBloom. New York was the last state with an inBloom partnership; shortly after the state ended this partnership, the corporation dissolved.[49]

The story of inBloom is a hopeful one as it demonstrates that those close to children, namely school administrators, teachers, and parents, hold values that are typically antithetical to the corporate appropriation and heedless technological disruption of the educational commons. As reflected in the growing opposition in the United States to the Common Core and the standardized-testing opt-out movement, most parents and teachers believe that education is fundamentally about human relationships that cannot be quantified, measured, standardized, predicted, and optimized by machines. However, with this said, digital technologies do have progressive functions and possibilities. Online and distance learning can provide access to education for students isolated due to disability or geography. If used thoughtfully, adaptive learning systems might also prove useful for teaching basic foundational knowledge such as memorizing the periodic table or mastering multiplication. Moreover, digital technologies may prove useful for decentering some aspects of scripted curriculum and standardization within public schooling, and provide ways of linking students to forms of engaged learning and problem-posing embedded within the community that align with their unique interests and passions. In this sense, algorithmic technology could aid in constructing new modes of educational commons that do indeed exceed the limitations of industrial-era schooling.

However, in their current dominant form, algorithmic learning technologies represent a form of "customized privatization" of the educational commons.[50] Imagining ways in which algorithmic education could enhance the emancipatory aspects of the educational commons would mean reformulating educational technology within a different set of values and sociotechnical imaginaries outside and beyond the logic of the neoliberal control society. Ultimately, the question we should be asking is not how digital technology can disrupt education (particularly for narrow economic purposes that serve powerful corporate interests), but how our communities and educational institutions can be supported and transformed to mobilize technology and generate technological literacies in line with progressive, democratic, and sustainable communities and futures.

Notes

1 I am not the first to coin the term "algorithmic education" and the term has been used by other education scholars: see for instance Carlo Perrotta and Ben Williamson. "The Social Life of Learning Analytics: Cluster Analysis and the 'Performance' of Algorithmic Education." *Learning, Media and Technology* (2016): 1–14.
2 Phil McRae. "Rebirth of the Teaching Machine through the Seduction of Data Analytics: This Time it's Personal." *National Education Policy Center*, April 30, 2013. Retrieved from http://nepc.colorado.edu/blog/rebirth-teaching-machine-through-seduction-data-analytics-time-its-personal
3 Richard Kahn and Douglas Kellner. "Paulo Freire and Ivan Illich: Technology, Politics and the Reconstruction of Education." *Policy Futures in Education* 5, no. 4 (2007): 440.

4   McRae, 2013.
5   Larry Cuban quoted in Neil Selwyn. *Is Technology Good for Education?* Cambridge, UK: Polity, 2016, 19.
6   See Heather Roberts-Mahoney, Alexander J. Means, and Mark J. Garrison. "Netflixing Human Capital Development: Personalized Learning Technology and the Corporatization of K-12 Education." *Journal of Education Policy* 31, no. 4 (2016): 405–420.
7   Selwyn, 2016, 109.
8   Kenneth J. Saltman and Alexander J. Means. "From 'Data-Driven' to 'Democracy-Driven' Educational Leadership: Navigating Market Bureaucracy and New Technology in a Post-Fordist Era." In Duncan Waite and Ira Bogotich (Eds.), *The Wiley International Handbook of Educational Leadership*, Malden, MA: Wiley Blackwell, 2017, 125–138.
9   Ibid.
10 Jennifer Medbery. "Reinventing Education to Teach Creativity and Entrepreneurship." *Fast Company*, May 1, 2012. Retrieved from www.fastcoexist.com/1679771/reinventing/education-to-teach-creativity-and-entrepreneurship
11 Gingrich quoted in Neil Selwyn. "Minding Our Language: Why Education and Technology Is Full of Bullshit ... and What We Can Do about It." Paper presented to the Digital Innovation, Creativity & Knowledge in Education conference, Qatar. Retrieved from www.academia.edu/9792417/Minding_Our_Language__why_education_and_technology_is_full_of_bullshit_..._and_what_might_be_done_about_it
12 Source: US Department of Education, Office of Educational Technology. "Enhancing Teaching and Learning through Educational Data Mining and Learning Analytics: An Issue Brief." October 2012, 30.
13 Audrey Waters. "The Algorithmic Future of Education." *Hack Education*, October 22, 2015. Retrieved from http://hackeducation.com/2015/10/22/robot-tutors
14 Ibid.
15 Selwyn, 2016.
16 Knowledge Works, which is profiled in the next section of this chapter, explicitly refers to inequality as a "design problem."
17 Max Weber. *From Max Weber: Essays in Sociology*. New York, NY: Routledge, 2009; Max Horkheimer, Theodor W. Adorno, and Gunzelin Noeri. *Dialectic of Enlightenment*. Palo Alto, CA: Stanford University Press, 2002.
18 Jürgen Habermas. *The Theory of Communicative Action*. Boston, MA: Beacon Press, 1985; Herbert Marcuse. *One-Dimensional Man: Studies in the Ideology of Advanced Industrial Society*. Routledge, 2013, 11.
19 Donna Haraway. *Simians, Cyborgs, and Women: The Reinvention of Nature*. New York, NY: Routledge, 2013; Sandra G. Harding. *The Science Question in Feminism*. Ithaca, NY: Cornell University Press, 1986; Chandra Talpade Mohanty. *Feminism without Borders: Decolonizing Theory, Practicing Solidarity*. Durham, NC: Duke University Press, 2003; Vandana Shiva. *Earth Democracy: Justice, Sustainability and Peace*. London, UK: Zed Books, 2016.
20 Kahn and Kellner, 2007, 432.
21 Wired Staff. "You Are a Cyborg." *Wired Magazine*, February 1, 1997. Retrieved from https://www.wired.com/1997/02/ffharaway/
22 Ben Williamson. "Silicon Startup Schools: Technocracy, Algorithmic Imaginaries and Venture Philanthropy in Corporate Education Reform." *Critical Studies in Education* (2016): 4–5.
23 Holman Jenkins Jr. "Google and the Search for the Future." *Wall Street Journal*, August 14, 2010. Retrieved from https://www.wsj.com/articles/SB10001424052748704901104575423294099527212

24 Williamson, 2016, 5.
25 All of the following information in this section comes from this document, which does not contain page numbers: Knowledge Works. "Recombinant Education: Regenerating the Learning Ecosystem." Knowledge Works Forecast 3.0. Retrieved from http://knowledgeworks.org/sites/default/files/Forecast3_0_0.pdf
26 Jeremy Rifkin. *The Zero Marginal Cost Society: The Internet of Things, the Collaborative Commons, and the Eclipse of Capitalism.* New York, NY: St. Martin's Press, 2014.
27 Ibid., 11.
28 Ibid., 19.
29 Steven Hill. "What Happens to Jobs in the Uber Economy?" *CNN*, October 22, 2015. Retrieved from www.cnn.com/2015/10/22/opinions/hill-jobs-in-new-economy/index.html
30 Cathy O'Neil. *Weapons of Math Destruction: How Big Data Increases Inequality and Threatens Democracy.* Lake Arbor, MA: Crown Books, 2016.
31 Christina Pazzanese. "Don't Trust that Algorithm." *Harvard Gazette*, October 16, 2013. Retrieved from http://news.harvard.edu/gazette/story/2016/10/dont-trust-that-algorithm/
32 Tech developers are thus busy finding new ways of embedding sensors and feedback mechanisms into the object world to track and monitor our behaviors and preferences. For instance, there are now IoT "smart toilet" prototypes that will catalogue, measure, assess, and provide detailed reports on the frequency and quality of your evacuations.
33 Evgeny Morozov. "The Rise of Data and the Death of Politics." *The Guardian*, September 19, 2014.
34 Ibid.
35 Julie Landry Peterson. "For Education Entrepreneurs, Innovation Yields High Returns." *Education Next*, no. 2, Spring 2014. Retrieved from http://educationnext.org/for-education-entrepreneurs-innovation-yields-high-returns/
36 Selwyn, 2016, 109.
37 Ibid., 110.
38 Peterson, 2014.
39 I have borrowed this example of Wayang Outpost from "Netflixing Human Capital Development," cited above, my co-written paper with Heather Roberts-Mahoney and Mark Garrison, 2016. This work was based on Heather's brilliant dissertation: "The Role of Big Data and the Privatization of Education." Unpublished PhD thesis, D'Youville College.
40 OECD. "Students, Computers, and Learning." Retrieved from www.oecd.org/education/students-computers-and-learning-9789264239555-en.htm
41 Sean Coughlan. "Computers 'Do Not Improve Results', Says OECD." *BBC*, September 15, 2015. Retrieved from www.bbc.com/news/business-34174796
42 Chris Rowan. "10 Reasons Why Handheld Devices Should be Banned for Children under the Age of 12." *Huffington Post*, March 7, 2017. Retrieved from www.huffingtonpost.com/crisrowan/10-reasons-why-handheld-devices-should-be-banned_b_4899218.html
43 Victoria Dunckley's analysis in *Psychology Today*, "Screentime is Making Kids Moody, Crazy, and Lazy," can be found here: https://www.psychologytoday.com/blog/mental-wealth/201508/screentime-is-making-kids-moody-crazy-and-lazy. I would also highly recommend a very detailed and useful annotated position paper and review of the health research on children and technology by the organization Parents Across America. "Our Children @Risk." Retrieved from http://parentsacrossamerica.org/wp-content/uploads/2016/07/Documentation6-29-16JW.pdf

44 Terry Moe and John Chubb. *Liberating Learning: Technology, Politics, and the Future of American Education*. San Francisco, CA: Jossey-Bass, 2009: 97.
45 McRae, 2013.
46 Linda Darling Hammond. "Education for Sale." *The Nation*, March 9, 2017. Retrieved from https://www.thenation.com/article/can-the-education-system-survive-betsy-devoss-extreme-school-choice-agenda/
47 Eames Yates. "This Silicon Valley School Shuns Technology—Yet Most of the Students Are Children of Tech Execs." *Business Insider*, March 23, 2017. Retrieved from www.businessinsider.com/waldorf-silicon-valley-school-shuns-technology-2017-3
48 Gilles Deleuze. "Postscript on the Societies of Control." *October* 59 (1992): 5. For a smart analysis of control societies and educational technology see Sam Sellar and Greg Thompson. "The Becoming-Statistic: Information Ontologies and Computerized Adaptive Testing in Education." *Cultural Studies ↔ Critical Methodologies* 16, no. 5 (2016): 491–501.
49 For a detailed record of the inBloom story see Class Size Matters. "inBloom and the Need to Protect Student Privacy." Retrieved from www.classsizematters.org/inbloom_student_data_privacy/
50 Roberts-Mahoney, Means, and Garrison, 2016.

6

AUTOMATION: DISPLACEMENT AND RUPTURE

As of July 2017, a Google News search of "robots" and "jobs" yielded more than two million stories. A small sample of the clickbait headlines:

- "Find Out if a Robot Will Take Your Job" (*Time*);
- "The Long-Term Jobs Killer Isn't China. It's Automation" (*New York Times*);
- "Are Robots Taking Over the World's Finance Jobs?" (*Huffington Post*);
- "Robots Could Dramatically Change the Nature of Retail Jobs" (*Business Insider*);
- "Rise of the Machines: The Future Has Lots of Robots, Few Jobs for Humans" (*Wired*);
- "Robots will Destroy Jobs and We Are Not Ready for It" (*The Guardian*);
- "Robots, Not Immigrants, Are Taking American Jobs" (*Los Angeles Times*).[1]

Alongside a growing number of popular books such as Erik Brynjolfsson and Andrew McAfee's *The Second Machine Age*, Martin Ford's *Rise of the Robots*, and Klaus Schwab's *The Fourth Industrial Revolution*, there has been a recent wave of speculation concerning automation and the future of work.[2] Just as machine learning and data platforms raise the possibility of replacing teachers and/or turning them into adjuncts of adaptive software, so too are jobs at risk of technological obsolescence in fields as diverse as fast food, truck driving, and financial analysis. Societies have long absorbed the idea of robots replacing standardized and repetitive factory jobs. However, the most common jobs in the United States today are retail sales assistant, food service worker, and office clerk, all of which, given emerging artificial intelligence, machine learning, and information software, are now highly susceptible to automation.[3] Recent studies suggest that anywhere between 50 and 80 percent of all job categories in the United States are at high risk of automation in the coming decades, and this includes service jobs as well as high-skilled, salaried professional positions.[4] We are only just beginning to think through the implications of what it might mean to have journalists, lawyers, medical specialists, and corporate accountants replaced by information software.

The idea that accelerating automation has the potential to wreak havoc on societies in the form of technological unemployment is now being widely debated. As Peter Frase notes, "the persistently weak post-recession labor market has produced a generalized anxiety about job loss. Automation and computerization are beginning to reach into professional and creative industries that long seemed immune ... and the pace of change at least seems, to many, to be faster than ever."[5] Alternatively, however, there is also a sense that automation contains utopian potential and could help create a better and more humane world that actually frees people from drudgery, or what David Graeber calls bullshit jobs (jobs that have little personal meaning and/or societal value other than a paycheck), while forming a socio-technical foundation for solving some of the world's most intractable problems.[6] A key question largely overlooked in the growing cottage industry of speculative books and articles is: What impact will automation have on the future of education?

Since the 1990s and the rise of the knowledge economy and cognitive capitalism, mainstream narratives have positioned education as a driver of economic progress and employment. For societies, it is popularly understood that by producing dynamic human capital endowed with high-end creative and technical capacities, education serves to boost the productivity of labor and therefore solve economic problems by ensuring jobs and endless growth. For individuals, educational investments and acquisition of credentials holds the promise of personal empowerment, a secure livelihood, and meritocratic self-realization. This chapter considers how such economic conceptions of education may increasingly lose coherence as technological displacement of labor tracks with stagnation, precarity, and inequality. The perspective adopted here is not an assertion that new technologies such as robotics, information software, and machine learning are rendering work obsolete, but rather that automation is a factor in the present erosion of livelihoods (i.e. jobs and employment). There will, of course, always be useful work to be done; however, it is uncertain—given some predictions regarding technological acceleration—what relation, form, and structure "education" and "jobs" will take in the future.

Creative Destruction: A Brief Cognitive Map

Concerns over the displacement of human labor by machines are as old as capitalism itself. A key touchstone is, of course, the Luddite rebellion against the power looms of the early nineteenth century. However, since the Industrial Revolution, economists have extensively debated whether technology can in fact generate long-term unemployment.[7] In the nineteenth century, economists such as J.S. Mill and David Ricardo argued that labor-saving technology could have a negative long-term impact on employment. In his *Principles of Political Economy and Taxation*, Ricardo observed that the "substitution of machinery for human labor is often injurious to the class of laborers ... [It] may render the population redundant and deteriorate the conditions of the laborer."[8] Others, such as John Baptiste Say, rejected the views of Mill and Ricardo. For Say, technology increases economic productivity and output, and therefore while it might displace workers in the short term, new forms of employment necessarily arise as demand grows to meet supply.

In his efforts to deepen Ricardo's analysis and at the same time refute Say's assertion that supply creates its own demand, Marx located the drive to replace workers with machines as internal to capitalism and its fundamental contradictions. In the *Grundrisse*, Marx observed that "the increase of the productive force of labor and the greatest possible negation of necessary labor is the necessary tendency of capital ... the transformation of the means of labor into machinery is the realization of this tendency."[9] Coercive inter-firm competition over market share induces a constant pressure to reduce operating costs and enhance productivity through labor-saving innovations. This "necessary tendency" to substitute machinery (fixed capital) for labor (variable capital) is part of what gives capitalism its technological dynamism. However, as capital outwardly expands and innovates, Marx argued, the technological displacement of workers threatens to produce a falling rate of profit, largely because redundant workers lack the requisite purchasing power to spur necessary levels of consumption. In this sense, technological change contributes to undermining capitalism in the long run, while at the same time Marx suggested that it provided a rational-technical foundation for socialism.

In the twentieth century, the conservative Joseph Schumpeter explicitly developed his concept of "creative destruction" out of Marx's insights. However, for Schumpeter, a key driver of innovation absent in Marx's thought concerns the role of the "entrepreneurial function" within capitalism, which involves a generative process of building upon and recombining pre-existing forms of knowledge and technology.[10] "The function of the entrepreneurs," he writes, "is to revolutionize the pattern of production."[11] This occurs "by exploiting an invention or, more generally, an untried technological possibility for producing a new commodity or producing an old one in a new way."[12] While this process leads to the obsolescence of older forms of production and labor, Schumpeter argued, it simultaneously drives expansion of consumption and employment.

Interestingly, despite his views on entrepreneurship and innovation, Schumpeter shared Marx's pessimism regarding the long-term viability of capitalism. However in his view socialism would eventually prevail not because of economic failure derived from the immiseration of the worker, but due to a stifling of the "entrepreneurial function" via the growth of a bureaucratic state governed by "trained specialists" and economic managers. In many respects, this was precisely the administrative future of capitalism anticipated by Schumpeter's contemporary John Maynard Keynes, but with a more optimistic outlook on the future. In his essay "Economic Possibilities for Our Grandchildren," Keynes predicted that in the twentieth century automation would eventually outpace job creation and cause widespread "technological unemployment."[13] However, while Keynes argued that this might prove disruptive in the short term, he predicted that the negative consequences could be offset through enlightened state planning, a reduction of working hours across the population to a 15-hour work-week, and the public reinvestment and redistribution of capital surpluses derived from increasing efficiency and productivity.

Needless to say, the predictions of Marx, Schumpeter, and Keynes have not come to pass. Marx could not anticipate the Keynesian compromise between capital and labor that emerged in the mid-twentieth century, which ensured steady growth through state-managed wage and benefit guarantees for a growing middle class, employed not just in industry but in a whole new stratum of salaried administrative and managerial positions. Similarly, neither Keynes nor Schumpeter foresaw the return to market fundamentalism and the triumph of neoclassical economic doctrine as the postwar settlement between capital and labor unraveled in the 1970s.[14] Putting these historical ironies aside, it has, of course, been Schumpeter rather than Marx or Keynes who has carried the day in mainstream economics when theorizing the relationship of technology and employment.

Over the past four decades, the prevailing view in mainstream economics has taken its cues from Schumpeter, thus rejecting the "Luddite fallacy" that labor-saving technology destroys jobs.[15] Since market forces and new technologies have historically generated many more new jobs than they have destroyed, the belief is that this pattern can and will continue indefinitely into the future. Based on this assumption, mainstream economists, meaning those fashioned in the neoclassical mold, have come to hold a stolid consensus on two key conceptual points: (1) the efficient markets hypothesis, or the notion that if left undisturbed, aggregate exchanges within self-regulating markets always tend toward equilibrium and full employment; (2) marginal productivity, which suggests employment and income are determined by supply and productivity of labor (output per worker) based on human-capital factors related to the level of educational development.[16] Drawing on these principles, it is argued that human-capital upgrades through education inherently drive economic growth and full employment, while reducing wealth and income inequality over time. However, since the 1970s, and despite rising post-secondary attainments, there has been a steady decline in economic growth and weak labor-force participation rates across highly developed economies such as the United States.[17] Moreover, since the 1970s, and contrary to marginal productivity theory, there has been a weakening in the relationship between productivity and income distribution, which cannot be attributed simply to differences in education and skill, as the fruits of technological innovation and economic growth have been appropriated overwhelmingly by the top 1 percent.[18] There are, of course, multiple complex factors driving stagnation and inequality across societies. Liberal economists such as Joseph Stiglitz, Robert Reich, and Paul Krugman, drawing on Keynesian perspectives, cite the intersection of weak effective demand, decline of unions, and the abandonment of "rational" economic management by a plutocratic corporate elite.[19] However, a growing number of economists, sociologists, journalists, and technology writers are pointing to automation of jobs as a key variable.

Automation and the New Jobless Future

Contemporary concerns over automation can be traced to the 1990s and the rise of globalization and the IT revolution. In this era, enhanced mobility of capital and production, automation, outsourcing, and the growth of service work, temporary contracting, and "symbolic analytic" labor began to speed up the displacement of Western manufacturing jobs, erode employment security, place downward pressure on wages, and reconfigure class, ethno-racial, and gendered divisions of labor. The acceleration of automation led some analysts, such as Stanley Aronowitz and William DiFazio, David Noble, and Jeremy Rifkin, to suggest that information technology and robotics threatened a "jobless future" and/or an "end of work."[20] Rifkin argued that history was entering a Third Industrial Revolution where "new, more sophisticated software technologies are going to bring civilization to a near workerless world ... by the mid-decades of the twentieth century."

While generating quite a bit of media buzz, these predictions were generally dismissed at the time. Channeling the ghosts of Say and Schumpeter, mainstream economists argued that automation might displace some jobs in the short term—especially those requiring low levels of education and skill, such as in agriculture and manufacturing—but in the long term, new high-paid, high-skilled jobs would be created in the knowledge economy and in the IT sector itself. This perspective on automation and future employment is now being widely reassessed even among elite economists and politicians such as those attending the World Economic Forum meetings in Davos, Switzerland. In 2015, the World Technology Network held the first world summit on technological unemployment in New York, featuring speakers such as Joseph Stiglitz, Martin Ford, and Robert Reich. The summit took a strong position on potential acceleration of automation:

> Accelerating technological unemployment will likely be one of the most challenging societal issues in the twenty-first century. Never before in history are so many industries being simultaneously upended by new technologies. Though "creative destruction," in which lost jobs are replaced with new ones, will be a factor, our newest technologies have the clear potential to eliminate many more jobs than we create. With technology advancing at a geometric pace, robotics, artificial intelligence, 3D-printing, and other innovations with enormous disruptive potential will soon hit the mainstream. Billions of people worldwide are currently employed in industries that will likely be affected—and billions of new entrants to the workforce will need jobs.[21]

The new "end of work" or "post-work" speculation often begins with the principle of Moore's Law, which observes that computing power has doubled roughly every 18 months since the mid-1960s. Named after Gordon Moore, a founder of Intel, Moore's Law suggests that information technology is accelerating at an exponential rate and thus intensifying innovation. In their widely discussed book *The Second Machine Age*, MIT economists Erik Brynjolfsson and Andrew McAfee follow Moore's Law to predict that we are on the verge of a revolution in machine learning and information technology that will dramatically transform employment in the decades ahead.[22] With breakthroughs in the capacity of machines to learn and self-improve through algorithms, a new generation of computers, programs, and apps can now perform previously unimaginable tasks. IBM's Watson supercomputer can handily outwit former *Jeopardy* champions. Google can translate the world's literary output into hundreds of languages instantly at zero cost. Software made by the company Automated Insights can write basic news and sports stories for the Associated Press. Brynjolfsson and McAfee are largely optimistic about the progress of Moore's Law. While millions of jobs may be displaced, technology also increases productivity and prosperity. In their view, the challenge of job loss can be met through a mix of innovative entrepreneurship and education investment.[23]

Martin Ford, a Silicon Valley software entrepreneur, makes similar observations. In his book *Rise of the Robots*, he suggests we are approaching a shift between workers and machines, where intelligent machines transition from being tools for workers to becoming workers themselves.[24] In manufacturing, shipments of industrial robots grew by 60 percent between 2000 and 2012.[25] Robots are now able to program themselves, swap functions and tools as needed, and complete complex technical processes like building iPhones and iPads in China's Foxconn factories or high-performance Tesla vehicles at Elon Musk's high-tech factory in Fremont, California. Amazon's little orange Kiva robots can now manage most basic warehouse duties of moving and tracking packages with little human oversight. In transportation, driverless cars and trucks stand poised to potentially displace millions of drivers. In US trucking alone, 3.5 million professional drivers are at risk of being replaced by autonomous vehicles. In the service sectors, a San Francisco start-up called Momentum Machines has developed a scalable prototype of an automated kitchen to be used in fast food, food trucks, and vending machines. Ford argues that the "increased automation of the fast food industry is almost certainly inevitable," potentially threatening millions of low-wage workers who already have few alternatives to McDonald's or Taco Bell.[26]

Importantly, Ford argues that automation is poised to impact not only service and manufacturing jobs requiring low levels of education and skill, but also a stratum of professional jobs requiring advanced education and training. "Acquiring more education and skills will not necessarily offer protection against job automation in the future," he writes.[27] Ford uses the example of a radiologist who specializes in reading complex images to make medical diagnoses. These are high-paid experts that typically spend 13 or more years in advanced educational training. Ford documents that computers are getting better at reading images than the radiologists. "It's quite easy to imagine," he notes, "that in the not too distant future, radiology will be performed almost exclusively by machines."[28] For Ford, these developments signal profound challenges for the economy and society that only extensive redistributive policies such as a guaranteed basic income can ameliorate.

Recent empirical studies give weight to these post-work speculations. In a widely discussed study by University of Oxford economists Carl Frey and Michael Osborne, titled "The Future of Employment: How Susceptible Are Jobs to Computerisation?", the authors use sophisticated statistical modeling to examine 702 occupational categories, from emergency-management directors to insurance underwriters.[29] They estimate that over the next two decades, emergent technologies threaten to automate up to 47 percent of all job categories in the United States. This includes not only "routine" job categories that have traditionally been susceptible to automation, such as bank tellers and supermarket cashiers, but also "non-routine" categories requiring advanced machine-learning technology, such as legal research, journalism, telemarketing, and recreational therapy. Stuart Elliot of the OECD places these figures even higher. Using the same data but with different methods of analysis, he suggests that 80 percent of jobs are at risk of automation.[30] Below is a short list of some of the more surprising jobs that are at risk of automation:

Anesthesiologist: Johnson & Johnson recently introduced Sedasys, an automated sedation system that could remove those very highly paid human doctors from the operating room—and save hundreds of millions of dollars each year.
Butcher: A Japanese company has created robots that debone chickens and remove their breasts for meat at a rate ten times faster than humans, and more hygienically.
Hair-washer: A Panasonic bot that can discern the shape of a customer's head before beginning a scalp massage and hair wash went on trial in Japanese salons last year.
Taxi driver: Google is reportedly exploring how to turn its self-driving cars into "robo-taxis," autonomous vehicles that could pick up and ferry passengers on demand.
Financial journalist: An Illinois-based start-up has created an automated program that processes market data and produces financial news, mimicking human reasoning and writing.
Pharmacist: The health-services corporation McKesson markets an automated program that fills prescriptions, restocks medications, and keeps pharmacy records, reducing human error and medication costs.
Carpenter: MIT's IkeaBot can assemble notoriously confounding DIY Ikea furniture all on its own. If you prefer a more unusual style, a German chainsaw-wielding lumberjack robot makes a table-and-chairs set from scratch.
Stand-up comedian: "Data," developed by a Carnegie Mellon University researcher, measures audience laughter and applause in order to choose its next punchline.[31]

There are, of course, automation skeptics, who typically point to low productivity numbers as a sign that automation is not as pervasive as some suggest. If robots are replacing workers, they argue, then there should be measurable gains in productivity. Robert Gordon, an economist at Northwestern University, observes that in comparison to the big inventions of the industrial era like the steam engine and the railroad, the digital revolution has had a much smaller impact on economic productivity.[32] For Gordon, this is reflected not only in low productivity, but also in more general economic stagnation. Matthew Yglesias of *Vox* and Doug Henwood of the *Left Business Observer* also point to low productivity as evidence that robots are not actually displacing large numbers of jobs.[33] However, there are mainstream economists, such as Brynjolfsson and McAfee, who suggest we just haven't yet seen the big gains in productivity promised by the digital revolution and Moore's Law and anticipate this will change in the coming decades. Former US Treasury Secretary Lawrence Summers simply points to collapsing labor-force participation rates as evidence that automation is having an impact. The percentage of adults disengaged from employment in the United States, and who have given up looking for work altogether, is at an all-time high.[34] For instance, Summers details that for each male worker between the ages of 25 and 55 officially counted as "unemployed" in the United States, there are at least three others of working age that have given up looking for work and are thus not reflected in the official unemployment rates.[35] Moreover, Summers argues that this round of creative destruction may be different than in the past and that its impact may be far more rapid and disruptive than the agricultural or industrial revolutions. He observes:

> A generation from now, taxis will not have drivers; checkout from any kind of retail establishment will be automatic; call centers will have been automated with voice-recognition technology; routine news stories will be written by bots; counseling will be delivered by expert systems; financial analysis will be done by software; single teachers will reach hundreds of thousands of students, and software will provide them with homework assignments customized to their strengths and weaknesses; and on and on ... there are many reasons to think the software revolution will be even more profound than the agricultural revolution. This time around, change

will come faster and affect a much larger share of the economy. Workers leaving agriculture could move into a wide range of jobs in manufacturing or services. Today, however, there are more sectors losing jobs than creating jobs. And the general-purpose aspect of software technology means that even the industries and jobs that it creates are not forever.[36]

Mainstream economic doctrine tells us that as technology expands and displaces workers, new employment opportunities arise as technology and innovation create new markets and generate growth through rising productivity. However, in their book *Race against the Machine*, Brynjolfsson and McAfee provide data from the United States Bureau of Labor Statistics that shows the 2000s were the first decade on record in which net job growth in the United States was zero, and when accounting for population gains, 18 million new jobs would have had to be added in 2010 to match the total at the beginning of the decade.[37] Additionally, multiple studies indicate that as the number of middle-income jobs has declined, there was no net increase in high-paid, high-skill jobs in the knowledge sector, contrary to widespread predictions.[38] Moreover, while economists are divided on the relationship between the digital revolution and its relative contribution to productivity, jobs, and growth, it is nonetheless indisputable that since the 1970s productivity has slowly but steadily increased alongside GDP, while at the same time economic growth rates and real incomes have stagnated. Among other things, these trends appear to indicate that employers have been replacing workers with machines and information software, while, as Thomas Piketty has detailed in his book *Capital in the Twenty-First Century*, a small percentage of elite owners, investors, and executives are capturing an ever higher percentage of the economic value generated across the global economy.[39] According to Oxfam International, the global imbalances between capital and labor are becoming so stark that as of the year 2016 the world's richest 1 percent had a combined wealth greater than the bottom 99 percent of the world's total population. Automation is thus radically expanding the power of capital over labor.[40] John Lanchester illustrates this asymmetry in relation to the world's most profitable corporation, Apple:

> In 1960, the most profitable company in the world's biggest economy was General Motors. In today's money, GM made $7.6 billion that year. It also employed 600,000 people. Today's most profitable company [Apple] employs 92,600. So where 600,000 workers would once generate $7.6 billion in profit, now 92,600 generate $89.9 billion, an improvement in profitability per worker of 76.65 times ... this is pure profit for the company's owners, after all workers have been paid. Capital isn't just winning against labor: there's no contest.[41]

A future in which intelligent machines increasingly displace workers would present a number of sobering challenges and contradictions. As Keynes and Marx clearly recognized, an increasingly automated economy is a problem for capitalism largely because redundant workers lack the purchasing power to fuel the consumption necessary to promote endless growth. Deepening technological unemployment, if it were to happen, would thus aggravate economic stagnation due to a tendency toward overaccumulation—defined as a surplus of capital, productive capacity, and labor, alongside a scarcity of opportunities for profitable reinvestment. This is problematic not simply from the standpoint of political economy and jobs for workers, but also for maintaining a modicum of social and economic justice. As Peter Frase notes, "who benefits from automation, and who loses, is ultimately not a consequence of robots themselves, but who owns them."[42] As Frase rightly argues, this is a *political* rather than simply an *economic or technological* problem. We could imagine a society in which the fruits of ownership, productivity, and efficiency generated by new technology were broadly shared within egalitarian rather than plutocratic terms. Conversely, we could just as easily imagine a society in which a tiny few own, control, and appropriate the wealth produced by technology at the expense of the many. Both scenarios have been grist for countless utopian and dystopian novels, from Edward Bellamy's *Looking Backward 2000–1887* to Kurt Vonnegut's *Player Piano*. While the future is unpredictable, part of its uncertainty rests in our capacity to imagine what it could become rather than resign our fate to the ossified patterns set forth in the present.

Educational Ruptures

Despite the digital stormclouds, mainstream economists remain steadfastly committed to the distributional laws of self-regulating markets and marginal productivity. Here two lines of thought are typically offered in relation to accelerating automation. First, mainstream economists such as Tyler Cowen, Brynjolfsson and McAfee, and Lawrence Summers each acknowledge that automation may indeed prove profoundly disruptive and will most likely increase social and economic inequality in the years ahead. However, they also suggest that machine learning and information technology will bring unexpected benefits in addition. Innovation will make commodities cheaper by driving down costs of production and distribution. The negative effects of automation can be offset through the proliferation and consumption of cheap goods and services, new digital gadgetry, and distractive entertainment such as immersive video games. As human desires are unlimited, the theory tells us, so too are the potential market niches to serve these desires.

Second, mainstream economists suggest education and human-capital upgrading can continue to promote economic growth and offset some of the most disruptive consequences of automation by enhancing the capacities of workers to complement machines, garner a "wage premium," and invent the jobs of the future. However, a steady increase in technological unemployment, if it were to come to pass, would likely delegitimize narratives that position education as the primary solution for achieving economic security and prosperity for individuals and societies. Such narratives are built on a synthesis of neoclassical theories of human-capital investment and endogenous growth that now animate education policy and rhetoric. They also reflect the idea of skills-biased technological change discussed in Chapter 3, which suggests that economic growth, employment, and wages are heavily dependent on the capacity of formal education to provide the human-capital requirements demanded by technological change.

The turn to neoliberalism and the knowledge economy in the 1980s and the 1990s was supposed to provide a new terrain of upward mobility and high wages for workers, particularly those properly invested in developing their human capital through educational training for new forms of cognitive and creative labor such as in new IT services and the financial sectors. In their book *The Global Auction*, Phillip Brown, Hugh Lauder, and David Ashton argue that for most Western workers outside a small elite, this neoliberal "opportunity bargain," based on advanced human-capital education for secure employment, has increasingly proven to be a "false promise."[43] In their research, Brown, Lauder, and Ashton analyzed transnational data and interviewed more than 200 corporate managers, business executives, and state policy makers across many nations in Europe, North America, and Asia. They observe that as global educational systems have begun to catch up to the West, the world is now flooded with cheap high-skilled and low-skilled labor. Transnational corporations are in a commanding position over labor and can exploit the cheapest workers wherever they are located. In a global economy flush with low-cost workers, where capital mobility and new technologies are driving down labor demand and wages, the promise that "learning equals earning" is being upended.

> What the few can achieve the majority cannot regardless of how educated they are. Wage inequalities cannot be narrowed through better education or increasing skill levels because the global labor market is congested with well-educated, low-cost workers. Rather than an "age of human capital," where the economic successes of individuals and whole economies depend on how extensively and effectively people invest in themselves, human capital is subject to the law of diminishing returns. The claim from neoliberal economists that the supply of well-educated workers would create its own demand as employers seek to profit from more productive employees seems fitting to a different world.[44]

Accelerating automation stands to exacerbate these trends, creating a potential crisis of legitimacy for educational systems and the neoliberal rationalities that have shaped their purpose and value over the past few decades. Currently, the erosion of livelihoods and the belief in education as a meritocratic tool of upward mobility are fueling intensive competition for economic advantage. For instance, salaried professionals are now making unprecedented investments of time and money into developing the social, cognitive, and cultural capital of their children.[45] They do so through the purchase of exclusive real estate, which eases entrance to the best and most elite public and private schools; phalanxes of language and mathematics tutors; and enriching experiences that build their children's resumes, such as alternative spring break trips to build houses for the poor in Guatemala. Affluent young people are given these advantages so that they may outcompete their rivals further down the class structure by acquiring the right mix of relentless drive, diversified interests and activities, and just the right plucky air of entrepreneurial employability to access the slots in elite universities considered prerequisites to attaining internships and well-remunerated work in the new economy.

Salaried professionals are, of course, not the only group seeking to leverage education, as young people across the class structure have dutifully internalized the narrative that "learning equals earning." However, as Randall Collins observed in his study of *The Credential Society*, the competition over positional advantage for employment drives an arms race over educational attainment that produces diminishing returns on investment in the form of degree inflation.[46] As the number of individuals seeking and attaining higher-education degrees rises over time (US enrollment in degree-granting post-secondary institutions increased by 21 percent between 1994 and 2004 and by 17 percent between 2004 and 2014), the status and value of each degree awarded is reduced.[47] This occurs because the higher the number of degrees awarded, the more competition there is among degree holders for employment opportunities at any given level in the labor market. Moreover, as increasing numbers of young people seek to complete post-secondary education, employers respond by raising their minimum educational requirements as screening or filtering mechanisms. Collins argues that this occurs despite the fact that work-related skills are not typically set by the demands of technology, or learned in educational settings, but are rather acquired on the job and/or through informal networks.

Collins has recently written a powerful essay, titled "The End of Middle Class Work: No More Escapes," in which he argues that mass technological unemployment is an imminent threat to the middle class and ultimately to capitalism itself.[48] However, perhaps counterintuitively, Collins suggests that the expansion of education may actually provide a temporary "escape valve" for policy makers as a means to assuage some of the most disruptive consequences of technological unemployment in the coming years. Rather than simply reflect and/or reproduce intensifying competition and class stratification, Collins observes that educational expansion may act as a form of "hidden Keynesianism" that deflects and absorbs the insecurities associated with advancing automation and precaritization of employment. First, formal education functions as a mass public-works project employing large numbers of educators, administrators, and service and auxiliary personnel (these workers are nonetheless at risk of obsolescence from the digital integration of virtual learning, MOOCs, and adaptive learning systems), which pumps money into otherwise flagging economies. Second, educational expansion restricts the flow of labor into the employment sector, thereby keeping formal rates of unemployment and underemployment artificially low. One would be tempted to add here that educational expansion is also an increasing source of profit within a stagnating real economy, both directly, through the widespread privatization of educational services, and indirectly, through the financialization of tuition through student debt. Collins notes:

> Educational expansion is virtually the only legitimately accepted form of Keynesian economic policy, because it is not overtly recognized as such. It expands under the banner of high technology and meritocracy—it is the technology that requires a more educated labor force. In a roundabout sense this is true: it is the technological displacement of labor that makes school a place of refuge from the shrinking job pool, although no one wants to recognize that fact. No matter—as long as the number of those displaced is

shunted into an equal number of those expanding population of students, the system will survive.[49]

The problem of educational expansion as "hidden Keynesianism" is that it runs up against funding barriers as government budgets are squeezed from multiple angles in a time of stagnation and austerity. Additionally, as students take on growing levels of debt in order to secure and fund their access to higher education, families will continue to expect and demand a high rate of return on investment that governments and the economic system will be unable to provide. Further, as societies and individuals engage in the same tactics to gain competitive advantage, education is implicated in diminishing returns on investment. For instance, it is now common to observe that a college diploma is the new high-school diploma—a prerequisite for entry into even the lower strata of the labor market. Over time, the value of a four-year college degree may also decline as the numbers of individuals attaining them increase. Rather than a catalyst for limitless individual upward mobility, human capital adheres to the logic of scarcity, whereby inflation of credentials is used to *artificially create barriers to entry* for desirable job opportunities. Eric Olin Wright describes how the logic of scarcity is amplified by "opportunity hoarding"—i.e. embedded restrictions on the supply of the highly educated.

> High levels of education generate high income in part because of significant restrictions on the supply of highly educated people. Admissions procedures, tuition costs, risk aversion to large loans by low-income people, and a range of other factors all block access to higher education for many people, and these barriers benefit those in jobs that require higher education. If a massive effort was made to improve the educational level of those with less education, this program would itself lower the value of education for those who already have it, since its value depends to a significant extent on its scarcity … While some of the higher earnings that accompany higher education reflect productivity differences, this is only part of the story. Equally important are the ways in which the processes

of acquiring education excludes people through various mechanisms and thus restricts the supply of people available to take these jobs.[50]

Alongside these mechanisms that limit the flow of lower-income students into higher education, social science research suggests that professional-class parents, even those with self-described progressive views, are prone to resist expansion and redistribution of social and educational resources, and/or strategies to improve class and racial integration in education, if it is perceived that these measures will diminish the advantages their own children maintain over working-class and historically marginalized ethnic and racial-minority groups. The massive inequality in educational funding between white middle-class communities and low-income communities of color in the United States reflects this longstanding historical phenomenon. In his book *Dream Hoarders*, Richard Reeves, a fellow at the Brookings Institution, argues that elites are not simply looking out for the best interests of their own children, but are erecting protective barriers to prevent those lower down the socioeconomic ladder from eroding the advantages their children enjoy.[51] They do so by overtly and tacitly supporting exclusionary school and neighborhood zoning policies, legacy admission preferences to elite schools, and occupational licensing barriers, as well as through the exercise of political influence. For instance, when the Obama administration attempted to enact a modest tax-based change to 529 College Savings Plans to help lower-income families afford college, Democratic legislators were bombarded with complaints and subsequently dropped the proposal. Thus the idea that education can function as a form of "hidden Keynesianism" must contend not only with the structural instabilities of capitalism, including potential for mass technological unemployment, but also with the ways in which such crises become articulated within educational systems through the class, racial, and gendered conflicts immanent to neoliberal social formations.

Post-Work Education

The limits of human-capital education and the intensification of the credential society signal that automation could fuel *a crisis of legitimacy* as the deeply engrained faith in economic advancement through education is questioned and thrown into doubt. At present, this legitimacy crisis is assuaged through the thin veneer of meritocracy provided by neoliberal tropes of market freedom and individual reward through the work ethic, interpreted increasingly as devotion to educational advancement for workforce preparation. Such discourses have the effect of using appeals to education as a means to privatize the structural conditions of stagnation and insecurity immanent to a potential employment crisis in global capitalism stemming from the advance of labor displacing technology. There are no guarantees that these narratives can be ideologically maintained as the promise of education for social mobility and security threatens to be permanently undone.

Simultaneously, advancing automation coupled with stagnation and rising inequality within global capitalism and across societies has generated an interesting conversation on potential alternatives. Mainstream economists such as Tyler Cowen, Brynjolfsson and McAfee, and Lawrence Summers, who recognize the scale of potential disruption of technological displacement, nonetheless cling to a sense of dystopian inevitability that the laws of self-regulating markets and marginal productivity should be allowed to operate unhindered no matter the consequences. In this perspective, there is little that societies and individuals can do other than to invest in formal education and upgrade their human capital to compete for a shrinking pool of secure employment opportunities. Creative responses are not only unthinkable but also undesirable in mainstream economic thought. Tyler Cowen, for instance, imagines a libertarian paradise where unfettered capitalism, education, and technology provide a framework for objectively differentiating the deserving few from the undeserving multitude. He notes:

> Think of it as a kind of digital social Darwinism, with clear winners and losers. Those with the talent and skills to work seamlessly with technology and compete in the global marketplace are increasingly rewarded, while those whose jobs can just as easily be done by foreigners, robots or a few thousand lines of code suffer accordingly ... We will move from a society based on the pretense that everyone is given a decent standard of living to one in which

people are expected to fend for themselves ... Much of the rest of the country will have stagnant or maybe even falling wages in dollar terms, but they will also have a lot more opportunities for cheap fun and cheap education. Many of these people will live quite well—especially those who have the discipline to benefit from all the free or nearly free services that modern technology makes available. Others will fall by the wayside.[52]

If such a digitally mediated tooth-and-claw version of the future is not appealing, other, more progressive economists, journalists, and technology writers advocate for resurrecting the views of Keynes on technological unemployment—namely, a redistribution of work hours and profits across the population. Post-Keynesian perspectives suggest that automation is not something to be feared or resisted; rather, it is something that can be harnessed to achieve a more efficient capitalism and a more humane foundation for work and society. This might include measures such as instituting a guaranteed basic income and reinvestment of capital surpluses from rising productivity into public projects and direct employment in sectors such as the green economy. The idea of a guaranteed basic income is central here. Basic-income schemes have some ideological flexibility, as they are not only a cause championed by post-Keynesian thinkers but have also been offered by conservatives such as Friedrich von Hayek and Charles Murray, who view them as a more efficient and cost-effective approach to traditional welfare policy.[53]

However, basic-income models, whether progressive or conservative, require robust state action to redistribute wealth produced under capitalism. This is simply off the table for most mainstream economists and politicians, particularly in the United States, where progressive taxation is increasingly framed as inherently illegitimate and a drag on prosperity (the "job creators" will go on strike!), while any hint of redistributive income transfers is considered a dependency-breeding moral violation of the highest order. This is why Randall Collins makes a solid case that educational expansion is the most likely near-term response to potential intensification of automation in the United States, despite the actual limitations of human-capital education as an economic engine and driver of employment.

There is also a growing body of radical perspectives on the post-work society. These theories more or less accept that advancing automation would require instituting post-Keynesian reforms in the short term, such as a guaranteed basic income and systems of work sharing. However, where they depart is that they question the long-term viability and/or desirability of capitalist work arrangements, as well as capitalism itself as a system of production and distribution. Writers like Paul Mason, Peter Frase, Nick Srnicek, and Alex Williams each suggest that automation could conceivably contribute to producing a society beyond capitalism, based on techno-abundance and social equality.[54] However, realizing such a post-work society would be dependent on constructing a new politics and "common sense" in relation to political economy, technology, and the future that pushes beyond both mainstream and Keynesian ideas. I will come back to these perspectives on postcapitalism in relation to educational futures in the next chapter. Here I simply want to point out that radical perspectives are unique not simply because they offer critiques of capitalism, but because they also identify a need to redefine the very meaning of work.

Work is a central aspect of life. Work can be drudgery. It can also be a source of deep fulfillment. Under capitalism, one's livelihood, social status, and sense of self are inextricably bound to work. And for most people outside a small elite of owners and successful entrepreneurs, work is defined as a salaried or hourly waged job. To be out of work and unemployed under capitalism is to be a failed subject. It is to be stigmatized and rendered abject. The social and psychological consequences are well documented. To illustrate, consider the findings of a 2015 study by Princeton professors Anne Case and Angus Deaton that documents rising mortality rates among the white working class in the United States without a college degree.[55] A stunning collapse in labor-force participation among this group has generated a profound loss of stability. Rates of family breakdown and divorce, suicide, depression and anxiety, and alcohol and drug use have all skyrocketed alongside economic dispossession, leading to what Case and Deaton refer to as early "deaths of despair." Moreover, and importantly, this is a highly racialized phenomenon. Mortality rates of whites with no more than a high-school degree were 30 percent lower than mortality rates of blacks in 1999. In 2015, they were 30 percent higher. One explanation is that in an era in which the United States elected its first black president, this phenomenon reflects a psychosocial status anxiety stemming not only from the loss of jobs and economic security, but also from an additional perceived loss of what W.E.B Du Bois evocatively referred to as "the psychological wages of whiteness."[56]

In her insightful contribution *The Problem with Work*, Kathi Weeks draws on autonomist Marxism and feminism to argue that any viable conception of a humane post-work society requires a fundamental rethinking of work in order to free us from the social and psychological burdens it carries under capitalism.[57] For Weeks, we first need to begin by refusing the separation of economy and polity under liberalism, which is reflected in mainstream economic theories that view markets as autonomous from society and thus outside history. This separation depoliticizes the sphere of work and the work ethic by framing them as natural and spontaneous orders beyond ethical and political consideration. This is precisely what animates the sense that there are no alternatives to market fundamentalism—typified by Cowen's celebration of digital social Darwinism.

The *refusal of work* that Weeks advocates is, importantly, not a rejection of productive human activity, but of the specific way in which capitalism attenuates and limits the full range and potentiality of our individual and collective labor and action. It does so by valorizing only those forms of work oriented to the production of value for capital. In this sense, refusal is a valorization of human activity outside capitalism and a verification of the intrinsic creativity and generative force of human labor, knowledge, and cooperation.

One could imagine here a conception of work that explicitly rewards forms of labor that have social value, such as those forms that have been historically feminized under capitalism—caring for children, contributing to community, protecting the environment, and so on. Capitalism has no method of indexing and/or rewarding the inherent value of such work. Quite the opposite—as David Graeber perspicuously observes, there appears to be a direct inversion of how work is remunerated and valued relative to its social contribution.[58] For instance, while hedge-fund managers rake in billions of dollars playing juvenile games with money that add zero productive value to the economy or society, teachers, social workers, artists, and the like barely scrape by. Worse, they are blamed and stigmatized for their own debt and insecurity through the logic that they should have invested in more lucrative choices, such as becoming a hedge-fund manager, rather than dedicating their lives to serving others and adding to the commonweal.

If the technological displacement of employment accelerates, as some predict, it will only heighten these contradictions, along with the necessity to rethink the value and purpose of work in relation to education and the future. Clearly, education has a value that cannot be quantified and measured simply by returns to investment and GDP growth. Education has a humanizing potential and can provide edification not only to individuals, but also to collective life more broadly. As Martin Ford suggests, a basic income could free people from the negative consequences of technological unemployment by providing the time and incentives for individuals and communities to pursue more education, not simply as a means of economic utility maximization, but in order to develop our creative and intellectual capacities for producing meaning and value across all aspects of society. "The general idea," he writes, "is that we should value education as a public good. We all benefit when more people around us are more educated; this generally results in a more civil society."[59] In this sense, a guaranteed income funded through the redistribution of wealth generated by technological innovation and automation could find synergy with the development of educational cultures and institutions that enhance meaning and produce social value outside and beyond the strictures of capitalist work arrangements.

A new work ethic that connects a basic income to education for social value is one possible alternative framework to the human-capital logics that define mainstream educational policy and economic ideology. Automation could be leveraged to create a future in which individuals are liberated to pursue deeper forms of learning, engage in creative activity, and add value across the society. Such a vision of a *post-work learning society and educational culture* could take many interesting forms connected to different expressions of the future. Its realization would require a new mode of politics and common sense, and this would entail a broader transformation of values. While the future is inherently contingent and unknowable, predictions of technological acceleration throw the reductive orthodox human-capital matrix of education for employment into disarray, and with it the mainstream economic rationalities upon which the legitimacy of the neoliberal project depends. Ultimately, this may present an exciting opportunity to develop a new rational-technical and liberatory educational foundation for a post-work society to come.

Notes

1 David Johnson. "Find Out if a Robot Will Take Your Job." *Time*, April 21, 2017; Claire Miller. "The Long-Term Jobs Killer Isn't China. It's Automation." *New York Times*, December 21, 2016; Nafis Alam and Graham Kendall. "Are Robots Taking Over the World's Finance Jobs?" *Huffington Post*, June 29, 2017; Daniel Kline. "Robots Could Dramatically Change the Nature of Retail Jobs." *Business Insider*, June 29, 2017; Marguerite McNeal. "Rise of the Machines: The Future Has Lots of Robots, Few Jobs for Humans." *Wired*, June 2015; Dan Shewan. "Robots Will Destroy Jobs and We Are Not Ready for It." *The Guardian*, January 11, 2017; David Horsey. "Robots, Not Immigrants, Are Taking American Jobs." *Los Angeles Times*, March 31, 2017.
2 Erik Brynjolfsson and Andrew McAfee. *The Second Machine Age: Work, Progress, and Prosperity in a Time of Brilliant Technologies*. New York, NY: Norton, 2014; Martin Ford. *Rise of the Robots*. New York: Basic Books, 2015; Klaus Schwab. *The Fourth Industrial Revolution*. Geneva: World Economic Forum, 2016.
3 Derek Thompson. "A World Without Work." *The Atlantic*, July 5, 2015.
4 Carl Frey and Michael Osborne. "The Future of Employment: How Susceptible Are Jobs to Computerisation?" 2013. Retrieved from https://www.oxfordmartin.ox.ac.uk/downloads/academic/The_Future_of_Employment.pdf; Stuart W. Elliot. "Anticipating a Luddite Revival." *Issues in Science and Technology* 30, no. 3 (2014): 27–36.
5 Peter Frase. *Four Futures: Life After Capitalism*. New York, NY: Verso, 2016, 4.
6 David Graeber. "On the Phenomenon of Bullshit Jobs." *STRIKE! Magazine*, August 17, 2013.
7 Joel Mokyr, Chris Vickers, and Nicolas L. Ziebarth. "The History of Technological Anxiety and the Future of Economic Growth: Is This Time Different?" *Journal of Economic Perspectives* 29, no. 3 (2015): 31–50.
8 Ibid., 33.
9 Karl Marx. *Grundrisse*. New York, NY: Penguin, 1973, 693.
10 Joseph Schumpeter. *Capitalism, Socialism, and Democracy*. New York, NY: Routledge, 2003.
11 Ibid., 132.
12 Ibid.
13 John Maynard Keynes. "Economic Possibilities for our Grandchildren." 1930. Retrieved from www.econ.yale.edu/smith/econ116a/keynes1.pdf
14 See Wolfgang Streeck. *Buying Time: The Delayed Crisis of Democratic Capitalism*. New York, NY: Verso, 2014.

15 Alex Tabarrok. "Productivity and Unemployment." *Marginalist Revolution*, December 31, 2003. Retrieved from http://marginalrevolution.com/marginalrevolution/2003/12/productivity_an.html
16 John Bellamy Foster and Michael D. Yates. "Piketty and the Crisis of Neoclassical Economics." *Monthly Review* 66, no. 6 (2014): online.
17 Ibid.
18 Ibid.
19 See Robert Reich. *Beyond Outrage: What Has Gone Wrong with Our Economy and Our Democracy, and How to Fix It*. New York, NY: Vintage, 2012; Joseph E. Stiglitz. *The Price of Inequality: How Today's Divided Society Endangers Our Future*. New York: NY: Norton, 2012.
20 Stanley Aronowitz and William DiFazio. *The Jobless Future*. Minneapolis: University of Minnesota Press, 1994; David Noble. *Progress Without People: New Technology, Unemployment, and the Message of Resistance*. Toronto, ON: Between the Lines; Jeremy Rifkin. *The End of Work*. New York, NY: Tarcher/Putnam, 1995.
21 Quoted in Michael A. Peters. "Technological Unemployment: Educating for the Fourth Industrial Revolution." *Educational Philosophy and Theory* (2017): 1–6.
22 Brynjolfsson and McAfee, 2014.
23 Ibid., 10–11.
24 Ford, 2015.
25 Ibid., 3.
26 Ibid., 14.
27 Ibid., xv.
28 Ibid.
29 Frey and Osborne, 2013.
30 Elliot, 2014.
31 Elizabeth Ralph. "They Got This." *Politico*, November 2013. Retrieved from www.politico.com/magazine/story/2013/11/the-robots-are-here-098995
32 Robert J. Gordon. *The Rise and Fall of American Growth: The US Standard of Living since the Civil War*. Princeton, NJ: Princeton University Press, 2016.
33 Matthew Yglesias. "The Automation Myth." *Vox*, July 27, 2015; Doug Henwood. "Workers No Longer Needed?" *Left Business Observer*, July 17, 2015.
34 Lawrence Summers. "The Economic Challenge of the Future: Jobs." *Wall Street Journal*, July 7, 2014.
35 As of 2017, the official unemployment rate in the US has dipped below 4.5 percent, which is considered to be near the rate of full employment. However, this does not count the millions of people who have been out of work for longer than six months or who have given up looking for work altogether. For a conservative analysis of American economic precarity that calls into question the whole notion of "economic recovery" from the Great Recession for the working class see Nicholas N. Ebserstadt. "Our Miserable 21st Century." *Commentary Magazine*, February 15, 2017.
36 Summers, 2014.
37 Erik Brynjolfsson and Andrew McAfee. *Race against the Machine*. Lexington, MA: Digital Frontier Press, 2011, 35.
38 John Schmitt, Heidi Shierholz, and Lawrence Mishel. "Don't Blame the Robots: Assessing the Job Polarization Explanation of Growing Wage Inequality." *Economic Policy Institute*, 2013. Retrieved from www.epi.org/publication/technology-inequality-dont-blame-the-robots/
39 Thomas Piketty. *Capital in the Twenty-First Century*. Cambridge, MA: Harvard University Press, 2014.

40 Oxfam International. "An Economy for the 1 Percent." Oxfam Briefing Paper, January 18, 2017.
41 John Lanchester. "The Robots are Coming." *London Review of Books* 37, no. 5 (March 2015): 3–8.
42 Frase, 2016, 22.
43 Phillip Brown, Hugh Lauder, and David Ashton. *The Global Auction: The Broken Promises of Education, Jobs, and Incomes*. Oxford, UK: Oxford University Press, 2010.
44 Ibid., 12.
45 Sean F. Reardon. "The Widening Academic Achievement Gap between the Rich and the Poor: New Evidence and Possible Explanations." In Greg Duncan and Richard Murnane (Eds.), *Whither Opportunity?* Russell Sage, 2011: 91–116; Sean F. Reardon. "The Widening Income Achievement Gap." *Educational Leadership* 70, no. 8 (2013): 10–16.
46 Randall Collins. *The Credential Society: An Historical Sociology of Education and Stratification*. New York, NY: Academic Press, 1979.
47 National Center for Education Statistics. Retrieved from https://nces.ed.gov/fastfacts/display.asp?id=98
48 Randall Collins. "The End of Middle Class Work: No More Escapes." In Immanuel Wallerstein, Randall Collins, Michael Mann, Georgi Derluguian, and Craig Calhoun (Eds.), *Does Capitalism Have a Future?* New York, NY: Oxford University Press, 2013. 37–70.
49 Ibid., 54.
50 Eric Olin Wright. *Understanding Class*. New York, NY: Verso, 2015, 6.
51 Richard Reeves. *Dream Hoarders: How the American Upper Class Is Leaving Everyone Else in the Dust, Why That Is a Problem, and What to Do about It*. Washington, DC: Brookings Institution Press, 2017.
52 Tyler Cowen. "The Robots Are Here: Not Only Are They Taking Our Jobs, They Are Harbingers of a New Libertarian Age." *Politico*, November, 2013. Retrieved from www.politico.com/magazine/story/2013/11/the-robots-are-here-098995
53 The conservative version is a basic income that would replace all the other state safety net programs, such as in housing and food assistance. The idea is that a basic income places responsibility on individuals to provide for these safety nets in the marketplace rather than through the state. See Charles Murray. "A Guaranteed Income for Every American." *Wall Street Journal*, June 3, 2016.
54 Paul Mason. *Postcapitalism: A Guide to Our Future*. New York, NY: Penguin, 2015; Frase, 2016; Nick Srnicek and Alex Williams. *Inventing the Future: Postcapitalism and a World Without Work*. New York, NY: Verso, 2016.
55 Anne Case and Sir Angus Deacon. "Mortality and Morbidity in the 21st Century." Brookings Institution, March 23, 2017. Retrieved from https://www.brookings.edu/bpea-articles/mortality-and-morbidity-in-the-21st-century/
56 http://items.ssrc.org/beyond-the-wages-of-whiteness-du-bois-on-the-irrationality-of-antiblack-racism/
57 Kathi Weeks. *The Problem with Work: Feminism, Marxism, Antiwork Politics, and Postwork Imaginaries*. Durham, NC: Duke University Press, 2011.
58 Graeber, 2013.
59 Ford, 2015, 263.

7
FUTURITY: CAPITALISM AND MASS INTELLECTUALITY

The philosopher Giorgio Agamben has argued that the enclosure of the future has coincided with a reversal of cause and effect, whereby society is increasingly governed by reactive attempts to address second-order emergencies rather than causal processes.[1] The sociologist Ulrich Beck similarly refers to this as "reflexive modernization," where the effort to contain future risks emerging from our sociotechnical systems generate new problems to be managed, ad infinitum.[2] For example, there are geo-engineering projects in blueprint stage that envision blasting sulfur into the atmosphere to cool the earth's surface temperature as a means of combating climate change. The risks of technological intervention into the earth's climate processes vastly exceed simple carbon-pricing schemes and the socialized redistribution of proceeds back into green-energy investment. However, geo-engineering is, strangely, easier to imagine today than minor alterations to capitalism and its externalization of the social and environmental costs to endless growth.

Similarly, we cannot seem to imagine educational futures outside the narrow parameters set forth by twenty-first-century capitalism. Learning, technology, and the future are narrowly conceived as human capitalization to serve economic ends. Human capabilities from creativity, to design, to engineering, to communication are valued in terms of their potential contribution to economic productivity and growth. Problems such as automation of livelihoods and despoiling of the planetary bios are reconceived as educational problems to be addressed through market solutions and technological disruption of educational systems in the service of corporate and financial accumulation. These injunctions are based on ahistorical economic doctrine posing as objective science that cannot conceive of values outside the parameters of economic and technical calculation. This deflects attention from the sociopolitical foundations of global problems while diminishing the creative and innovative potential of educational systems for enacting alternative futures.

Silicon Valley and corporate imaginaries cannot imagine a future for educational organization and learning outside economic and digital determinism. This has a number of consequences. The first is in terms of *sociality*—precarity and inequality are said to reflect a failure of educational systems to adopt market solutions as well as a failure of persons to engage in gritty self-actualization through private human-capital investment. The second is in terms of *intellectuality*—learning is conceived as an individual and technical process of prescription narrowly channeled into "skills" to be optimized as opposed to an open, unpredictable, and intensively social process. The third is in terms of *agency*—rather than authentic creativity and transformation, human capability and action are reduced to learning for the sake of adaptation and resiliency to future shocks wrought by expansive historical and technological change. The fourth is in terms of *imagination*—the projection of possibility is restricted to visions of educational change at the level of marketization and new technology, but remains in stasis at the level of consciousness, ethics, and politics.

The rhetoric of human-capital education for twenty-first-century skills is couched in an ethos of problem solving and social justice, but the narrow structure of value in which it is embedded is holding back educational innovation and progress. Young people are told that *learning is for earning* and that the only possible means of addressing a future of insecurity and uncertainty is to develop an enterprise-self and invest in a personal "stock" of human capital to add value to the high-tech economy, or justly suffer the consequences. Never mind that the economy is largely producing low-wage service jobs that may soon be automated away, or that human capital and educational credentialism operate through dynamics of scarcity and diminishing returns. Moreover, this worldview is based in mainstream economic thought that obscures the class, race, and gendered power dynamics shaping global realities and social outcomes. As Thomas Piketty has detailed, growing economic inequality has more to do with plutocratic capture of decision-making and financial parasitism than with relative differences in talent, productivity, education, or skill. These "predatory formations," as Saskia Sassen calls them, are a reflection and driver of an ongoing systemic crisis of capitalism defined by stagnation and austerity.[3]

The subordination of education and, by extension, learning itself to capitalism is a distortion of educational value that erodes educational potential. As Tyson Lewis has observed, "not only has learning come to colonize schools and universities, but it has extended its reach beyond these institutions, transforming society as a whole into a kind of schoolhouse and workers and citizens into perpetual learners who must be continually schooled and re-schooled in order to remain competitive and flexible on an open market."[4] Of course, schools and universities are not businesses and human and intellectual development is not a commodity. When treated as such, those elements vital to educational creativity and knowledge production such as caring, reciprocity, mutuality, and cooperation are stunted. What might it mean to revalorize education? What would it mean to conceive of a new educational logic of futurity? To approach these questions, I believe it is first important to recognize that the future of education is intimately tied to the future of capitalism and the rationalities that sustain and define it in the present.

Futures of Capitalism

Capitalism is not a timeless fact of nature. It is a world-historical system. Like all historical formations, capitalism has different articulations and many potential futures. Capitalism today confronts an expansive set of structural challenges. The 2008 financial meltdown and Great Recession revealed long-term crisis tendencies that likely portend far deeper instabilities to come in the twenty-first century. One positive outcome has been a post-2008 revival of critical analysis and speculation on the future of capitalism. Even among elites, such as at the annual World Economic Forum meetings at Davos, questions concerning capitalism's future have moved front and center, particularly in light of growing inequality and the unpredictable impacts of new technology and climate change.

Across modern thought there has been broad agreement, even among the most strident critics such as Marx and Engels, that capitalism is a revolutionary engine of scientific and technological development. There has also been speculation that capitalism's technological foundation may eventually create the conditions for capitalism's transformation into a radically different form of political economy. Such ideas regarding the demise and transcendence of industrial capitalism are found, albeit in starkly different forms, in the thought of Marx, Schumpeter, Keynes, and Hayek.[5] They are also present in late twentieth-century analyses associated with the post-industrial society, knowledge society, information society, network society, and post-Fordism found in the work of thinkers such as Daniel Bell, Peter Drucker, and Antonio Negri, among others.

In light of the 2008 economic crisis and the collapse of neoliberal legitimacy stemming from what Yanis Varoufakis has called "the bonfire of financialization's illusions," new speculative analysis has emerged.[6] To begin, there is now wide speculation that capitalism has entered a period of indefinite *stagnation*. Mainstream economists such as Robert Gordon and Tyler Cowen suggest that capitalism has already reaped the productive benefits of major technological innovations and will see only minor benefits from the digital revolution, and is therefore consigned to a future of low productivity and growth.[7] Heterodox thinkers like Thomas Piketty, James Galbraith, John Bellamy Foster and Robert McChesney, while coming from very different economic perspectives, each conclude, the idea that high rates of economic growth can be maintained indefinitely is a dangerous fantasy, arising primarily in the post-World War II era due to specific historical circumstances that are unlikely to be replicated.[8] For these thinkers, capitalism contains inherent structural tendencies which make economic stagnation and extreme inequality a normal feature rather than an exception. They see a future for capitalism marked by endless crises and instability. Piketty argues for a global tax on wealth to address the most rapacious effects of capitalism. Galbraith argues for adapting capitalism to a long-term *low-growth* model of development. Bellamy Foster and McChesney argue for a socialist alternative to replace a stagnant capitalism.

In his 2017 essay collection, *The End of Capitalism*, Wolfgang Streeck argues that capitalism is not only stagnant, but undergoing a process of *disintegration*.[9] Streeck observes that Western capitalism entered a cycle of crises in the 1970s with the collapse of the postwar Keynesian social compact, which viewed democratic checks and redistributive compromises as economically productive. In its place arose what Streeck refers to as "neoliberal Hayekianism" predicated on total commodification of social life, the massive transfer of wealth from the bottom to the top of the class structure, and an assault on democratic authority reimagined as a drag on efficiency. For Streeck, the neoliberal triumph of capitalism over democracy has been a disaster not only for societies and citizens, but also for capitalism, manifested in stagnation, inequality, financial busts, and unsustainable public and private debt. He argues that capitalism is a victim of its own success having won a "pyrrhic victory" over those non-commodified spheres, values, and countervailing social forces necessary to sustain it in the long run. Streeck observes:

> Social systems thrive on internal heterogeneity, on a pluralism of organizing principles protecting them from dedicating themselves entirely to a single purpose, crowding out other goals that must also be attended to if the system is to be sustainable. Capitalism as we know it has benefited greatly from the rise of counter-movements against the rule of profit and of the market. Socialism and trade unionism, by putting a brake on commodification, prevented capitalism from destroying its non-capitalist foundations—trust, good faith, altruism, solidarity within families and communities, and the like.[10]

Streeck does not offer an alternative to capitalism, but instead argues that it has reached an interregnum, a period of long-term crisis and decay, and will eventually cease to exist entirely, replaced by an as-yet-unknown historical formation. "Eventually," he writes, "the myriad provisional fixes devised for short-term crisis management will collapse under the weight of daily disasters produced by a social order in profound, anomic disarray."[11] These daily disasters and anomic disarray include intensification of political instability driven by anger and disorientation in relation to a rapidly changing historical context and new threats to livelihoods, which has opened the door to right-wing demagogues like Trump and the slow evisceration of what remains of democratic norms and principles.

Others are more optimistic and predict a progressive *transcendence* of capitalism. Central here is the idea that digital technologies are creating new forms of cooperation and exchange that defy traditional proprietary arrangements and are thus undermining and transforming capitalism. In Chapter 5, I discussed the ideas of Jeremy Rifkin, who argues that a postcapitalist collaborative commons is emerging based on social entrepreneurship and sharing economy platforms, digital currencies, open-source software, commons licensing, and big data that are weakening profit models based on scarcity of knowledge and private monopoly over intellectual property.[12] Paul Mason makes similar arguments in his book *Postcapitalism*.[13] He observes that the transcendence of capitalism is possible due to three contemporary impacts of technology. First, automation is reducing the need for human labor and is eroding the links between work and wages. Second, the abundance of free information is eroding the capacity of markets to price goods correctly and is thereby circumventing capitalist proprietary frameworks. Third, the rise of collaborative production of goods and services is no longer strictly subject to external market demands and controls. However, unlike Rifkin, Mason does not view the transcendence of capitalism as a spontaneous historical inevitability, but rather the contingent and unpredictable outcome of looming social and political conflicts. He writes: "by creating millions of networked people, financially exploited but with the whole of human intelligence one thumb-swipe away, info-capitalism has created a new agent of change in history, the educated and connected human being."[14] He continues:

> The main contradiction today is between the possibility of free abundant goods and information and a system of monopolies, banks, and

governments trying to keep things private, scarce and commercial. Everything comes down to the struggle between the network and the hierarchy, between old forms of society molded around capitalism and new forms of society that prefigure what comes next.[15]

From a different angle, Nick Srnicek and Alex Williams, who are the most well-known recent advocates of the *acceleration* perspective, argue that rather than creating the conditions for transcendence, capitalism is constraining technological progress.[16] They note that "not only is capitalism an unjust and perverted system, but it is also a system that holds back progress … accelerationism is the basic belief that these capacities can and should be let loose by moving beyond the limitations imposed by capitalist society."[17] The ideological strength of neoliberalism, according to Srnicek and Williams, has been its success in presenting itself as synonymous with modernization, which is associated with consumer freedoms and innovations such as iPhones. However, neoliberalism presents an image of modernity that it is incapable of generating. Instead of liberating mass creativities and innovative freedoms through the abstract universalism of the market, neoliberalism places fetters on social and technological development. They write:

> Capitalism has begun to constrain the productive forces of technology, or at least, direct them towards needlessly narrow ends. Patent wars and idea monopolisation are contemporary phenomena that point to both capital's need to move beyond competition, and capital's increasingly retrograde approach to technology. The properly accelerative gains of neoliberalism have not led to less work or less stress. And rather than a world of space travel, future shock, and revolutionary technological potential, we exist in a time where the only thing which develops is marginally better consumer gadgetry. Relentless iterations of the same basic product sustain marginal consumer demand at the expense of human acceleration.[18]

Srnicek and Williams advocate for an alternative modernity driven by a techno-politics of acceleration. This would entail a radical-progressive movement aimed at accelerating capitalism's technological and innovative capacities and channeling them toward realization of sustainable, egalitarian, and democratic social formations. They suggest that "an accelerationist politics seeks to preserve the gains of late capitalism while going further than its value system, governance structures, and mass pathologies will allow."

Each of the perspectives outlined above on the future of capitalism harbors insights as well as complications, limitations, contradictions, and blind spots. Additionally, there are other important iterations of postcapitalism too numerous to map here, from the feminist community economics offered by J.K. Gibson-Graham to Hardt and Negri's multitudinal commonwealth.[19] Decolonial, green, and feminist perspectives importantly make central to postcapitalism the need to challenge systems of racism, patriarchy, and exploitation of nature and the environment inherent in capitalist modernization.[20] While aspects of stagnation, disintegration, transcendence, and acceleration are present in some form or combination in each of these iterations of postcapitalism, a general absence concerns analysis of education and learning in relation to the future of capitalism.

From Education as Capture to Mass Intellectuality

Stagnation, disintegration, transcendence, and acceleration are all distinct possibilities for capitalism in coming decades, leading to unpredictable sociopolitical formations. Crucial variables are the modes of education, learning, and consciousness that will shape the trajectory of capitalism and sociality in the twenty-first century. The future, of course, is not simply a question of political economy, but an articulation of prevailing educational and intellectual culture. The future of education has become a central preoccupation of mainstream economists, journalists, business leaders, and politicians who argue that new forms of learning are required to produce the enterprising subjectivities and technical capacities necessary to sustain twenty-first-century capitalism. We might suggest here that education is a problem for capitalism and capitalism is a problem for education. As the educational philosophers Jan

Masschelein and Maarten Simons have argued, capitalism is dependent not only on knowledge production and new technology, but on specific forms of learning—i.e. the transmission of entrepreneurial dispositions and productive skills directed at innovation for a digitized information economy.[21] However, the learning society cannot fulfill the task it sets out for itself. By subordinating educational institutions and social processes to markets and narrowing learning to prescriptive acquisition of "skills," the learning society denies the full expression of educational possibility and creativity, which is, paradoxically, what is said to be the basis of value and innovation in cognitive capitalism.

As I have argued in this book, the problem in education today is not located in the idea that we need new and more expansive forms of human capability and collaboration for the twenty-first century, but rather that our conceptualizations of educational value and purpose are being constrained by the triumph of markets and technology over ethics and sociality. We live in an age of enormous complexity and interconnection. It is also an age of stark regression as well as possibility. Obscene inequality, greed, racism, civic illiteracy, historical amnesia, and spiritual nihilism co-exist with new patterns of social innovation, engagement and activism, and the desire to build a common world. Within mainstream economic thought, unfettered capitalism and technology will enable endless growth, create endless high-paying jobs, and solve the world's social and ecological problems as long as human potential is transformed into human capital. This captures education and learning within a closed value system and is holding back progress and human capability.

A different logic of educational futurity would have to embrace alternative ways of conceiving education and society beyond their neoliberal reduction to twenty-first-century capitalism. To begin, I believe that educational researchers, educators, and educational activists need to denaturalize the prevailing economic assumptions that shape educational value and purpose in the present. Education is today valued mainly according to its contributions to economic growth, which has become the overarching measure of progress in the twenty-first century. If market fundamentalism is like a religion, then growth is the deity to which all must pay fealty including educational institutions, educators, and students. The idea that growth is an inherent good is so deeply engrained that to question it is to be perceived as a hopeless romantic, if not a heedless lunatic, clueless of the hard objective science of economics and the grim realities of human nature. However, GDP is an invention of industrial capitalism and only became central to conceptions of prosperity in the postwar era. It is not a law of nature, but a historical construct that traps us in a limited set of assumptions about what is possible for education and society. Douglas Rushkoff notes:

> We are caught in a growth trap. This is the problem with no name or face, the frustration so many feel. It is the logic driving the jobless recovery, the low-wage gig economy, the ruthlessness of Uber, and the privacy invasions of Facebook ... we are running an extractive, growth-driven operating system that has reached the limits of its ability to serve anyone, rich or poor, human or corporate. Moreover we are running it on supercomputers and digital networks that accelerate and amplify all its effects.[22]

The logic of economic growth presumes that on a planet with finite resources, technological efficiencies gained under capitalism, combined with the endless transformation of human potential into human capital, can ensure limitless prosperity and endless expansion of markets and consumption of natural resources. While economic growth under capitalism has produced immense wealth and raised living standards, it has also gone hand in hand with the erasure of Indigenous peoples and knowledge, worker exploitation and debt peonage, imperialism and militarization, and the destruction of land, air, soil, and wildlife. Moreover, economic growth says nothing about how wealth is distributed and/or how economic and social inequalities correlate with myriad global problems and lower levels of human health and happiness.[23] For instance, the United States is the wealthiest society in the world and yet it has some of the lowest measures of human wellbeing, reflected in scandalous rates of child poverty, family breakdown, depression and anxiety, addiction and despair, economic and racial segregation, and deep trust and empathy gaps. Moreover, despite what mass media trains us to believe, mass consumption does not improve quality of life either, and consumerism, as Tim Jackson notes, creates a value system totally detached from its social and environmental cost.[24]

What actually matters most for quality of life is not how wealthy a society is in either aggregate or relative GDP, but how unequal it is, particularly in relation to prevailing levels of social freedom and reciprocity. Synthesizing the social science research, Goran Therborn observes that inequality is toxic to the social fabric and squanders human capabilities:

> Inequality is a violation of human dignity; it is a denial of the possibility for everybody's human capabilities to develop. It takes many forms, and it has many effects: premature death, ill-health, humiliation, subjection, discrimination, exclusion from knowledge or from mainstream social life, poverty, powerlessness, stress, insecurity, anxiety, lack of self-confidence and of pride in oneself, and exclusion from opportunities and life-chances. Inequality, then, is not just about the size of wallets. It is a socio-cultural order, which (for most of us) reduces our capabilities to function as human beings, our health, our self-respect, our sense of self, as well as our resources to act and participate in this world.[25]

Inequality not only affects the poor; it impacts the rich. Studies demonstrate that in contexts of high inequality, the rich not only have a difficult time "empathizing" with the poor, but also show a predisposition to *anti-social attitudes*.[26] For instance, a study of 261 high-level corporate executives in the United States found that 21 percent had clinically significant psychopathology traits, including narcissism and absence of conscience. Only 1 percent of the general population exhibits such characteristics.[27] Christian Felber elaborates:

> We thrive when we live in accordance with human values: the building of trust, honesty, esteem, respect, empathy, cooperation, mutual help and sharing. The "free" market economy is based on the rules of the systematic pursuit of profit and competition.

> These pursuits promote egoism, greed, avarice, envy, ruthlessness and irresponsibility. This contradiction is not merely a blemish in a complex or multivalent world; rather, it is a cultural catastrophe; it divides us inwardly—as individuals and as a society.[28]

The idea that education can solve global problems by transforming persons into measurable units of human capital to promote GDP is a dead end for the future, based on false ideological premises. Competitive human-capital rationalities provide a justification for inequality and hold back economic, social, and technological innovation by conceiving human capabilities and potentials in reductive economic terms. We need a different set of referents to reimagine education and society beyond neoliberal prescriptions of human capital and GDP, which trap us in a narrow reality of commodification, self-blame, inequality, and technocratic objectification of reality. My view is that this requires a broader democratization of economic and social relationships wherein learning is made central to the task of achieving forms of prosperity evaluated and measured according to the realization of egalitarian and sustainable systems and relations.

First, we need a new language of freedom and equality. Market fundamentalism defines freedom as the right to buy and sell and equality as a dangerous fiction and/or violation of natural economic laws. The idea that freedom is a purely abstract economic capacity detaches human agency from a deeper sense of values and solidarity. The idea that inequality is simply an expression of individual choices and personal differences is similarly an ideological mystification, detached from realities of structure, domination, and power. In contrast, the philosopher Jacques Rancière has argued that equality is in fact an *a priori* truth.[29] Agency, difference, and freedom are the common elements of our equality. Inequality is a distortion of our common humanity and our capacity to collectively make and remake the world. Rather than value and measure education, learning, and social progress according to the austere logics of human capital and GDP, education should promote human flourishing by recognizing difference, freedom, and equality as the foundation of prosperity and community. We can call this idea *emancipation*. The language of emancipation does not depend on achieving identical outcomes for every individual in absolute terms, but presents a grounded ethos for imagining flourishing lives and self-determination for all regardless of individual differences in ability, gender, sexuality, race, ethnicity, or religion. As Noah De Lissovoy has insightfully elaborated, an *emancipatory education* requires decolonizing not only our schools and universities, but also the cultural valences of human knowing and being that define our sociality, values, and politics.[30] This moves us beyond a "thin" liberal construction of representation and tolerance, toward a "thick" notion of radical love that refuses all forms of fundamentalism, including misogyny, racism, and class exploitation.

Second, a language of emancipation prefigures a commitment to the *democratization* of economic and social relationships. We live in an era of plutocratic capture of politics enabled by an ideological separation of economics and democracy. Authentic democracy is not a model, an ideology, or a system of voting and representation. Rather, it is a contingent process, defined by competing interests and visions of the social, whereby power is vested in people's capacity for self-determination.[31] Democratic authority needs to be grounded in civil society based on values of reciprocity and the commonweal rather than the unlimited accumulation and concentration of private wealth and power. Markets, digital platforms, and technical capabilities need to serve people and communities rather than unaccountable state and corporate interests. Currently, new technologies, social media, social movements, and creative ways of organizing production, labor, and exchange are being imagined and put into practice in the United States and across the world. Some of these models directly challenge the proprietary foundations of capitalism, while others are attempts to embed economic activity and markets in democratic relationships. This includes proliferation of community development corporations, community land trusts, participatory budgeting, community schools, work-sharing arrangements, cooperatives and worker-owned enterprises, public reclamation of utilities and banking, and the greening of energy production. On a single street corner where I live in Buffalo, New York, in a low-income and racially and ethnically diverse neighborhood, four interlinked worker-owned cooperatives have sprouted up in the past few years. In response to growing inequality and precaritization of livelihoods, guaranteed basic income experiments are being conducted in places as diverse as Finland, India, California, Uganda, Canada, and Kenya. Grassroots movements for educational justice and equality are gaining strength as well.

Third, learning needs to be reconceived, from an instrumental process of standardization and prescriptive skill acquisition to one of authentic creativity and mass intellectuality. The complexity of global realities and challenges to human freedom and ecological sustainability are legion and require new intellectual and technical capabilities. A deep educational culture is central for realizing democratic futures. I refer to this as *mass intellectuality*. Mass intellectuality names the idea of education as a commons and shared capacity for critical thought and agency. To reorient educational value in terms of mass intellectuality is to suggest that there are alternative learning futures that can be actualized. Currently, there are proliferating conceptions of learning—learning society, deeper learning, blended learning, learning ecosystems, personalized learning, and adaptive learning to name a few. While these notions of learning call for dynamic human capabilities and problem solving for the twenty-first century, they primarily conceive of learning as an instrumental process of standardized, efficient, and prescriptive skill acquisition to serve the economy rather than authentic creativity and deep engagement with alternative futures.[32] In contrast, mass intellectuality emphasizes depth of transformative capability, collaboration, critical knowledge, and experimentation. This includes:

- *Systems integration*—the capacity of educational institutions, teachers, students, and communities to integrate fields of knowledge and directly link knowledge formation across economics, science, design, engineering, ecology, and technology to historical, philosophical, ethical, and political considerations;
- *Pattern recognition*—the capacity embedded in curriculum and pedagogy to synthesize, interrogate, and rework continuities, discontinuities, inconsistencies, and contradictions in complex flows of information, data, code, polemics, text, images, and affects across the

domains of science, media, humanities, arts and aesthetics, comparative politics, and social science;
- *Cognitive mapping*—the capacity to map interrelationships within and across various aspects of natural, urban, rural, and social geographies and realities and connect them to the historical modulations of capitalism, technology, and time;
- *Problem posing*—the capacity to assess history, experience, meaning, ideas, values, and practices through critical engagement with social, ethical, political, and ecological problems so as to reconstruct freedom and egalitarian relations;
- *Future modeling*—the capacity to creatively model utopian imaginaries that project radically different futures for education and society beyond capitalism and its reduction of history and culture to endless accumulation.

Mass intellectuality reflects a vision of education as a commons—a collaborative process and a social relation rather than as a machine to be optimized and calculated. It conceives of students as human beings, rather than as objects within a predictive input and output schema of economic skill acquisition for human capitalization of self, world, and other. Mass intellectuality names a process and set of capacities that integrates immanent social capacity with expertise and technical abilities. Language is important to consider here. How we describe the world matters. It shapes our reality and our sense of possibility. The regressive Right understands the mediated nature of politics better than the progressive Left. However, it offers a false promise of assuaging the harms of neoliberalism through a language of scapegoating, demagoguery, irrationalism, and nostalgic return to mythical community via blood-and-soil nationalism. Writing of the 1930s, Henry Farrell notes, "the more market crisis, the better fascism prospered, since it purportedly offered a way to re-embed markets within social structures, albeit at the cost of human freedom."[33] At its deepest level, democracy concerns the freedom and capacity of people and communities to determine the conditions of their own lives. This speaks to the centrality of a vibrant educational culture for realizing common democratic futures. The language of mass intellectuality, emancipation, and democratization describes an alternative value system to market fundamentalism and its attenuation of the future—a value system oriented to *truth and freedom* against the closure of *time and imagination*.

Notes

1. Giorgio Agamben. "For a Theory of Destituent Power." Public lecture in Athens, November 16, 2013. Retrieved from http://www.chronosmag.eu/index.php/g-agamben-for-a-theory-of-destituent-power.html
2. Ulrich Beck. *World at Risk*. Cambridge, UK: Polity, 2007.
3. Saskia Sassen. *Expulsions: Brutality and Complexity in the Global Economy*. Cambridge, MA: Belknap Press of Harvard University, 2014.
4. Tyson Lewis. *On Study: Giorgio Agamben and Educational Potentiality*. New York, NY: Routledge, 2013, 3.
5. See Matthew MacLellan. "Capitalism's Many Futures: A Brief History of Theorizing Post-Capitalism Technologically." *Mediations* 26 (2013): 159–179.
6. Yanis Varoufakis. "We Need an Alternative to Trump's Nationalism. It Isn't the Status Quo." *The Guardian*, January 22, 2017.
7. Tyler Cowen. *The Great Stagnation: How America Ate All the Low-Hanging Fruit of Modern History, Got Sick, and Will (Eventually) Feel Better*. A Penguin eSpecial from Dutton. Penguin, 2011; Robert J. Gordon. *The Rise and Fall of American Growth: The US Standard of Living since the Civil War*. Princeton, NJ: Princeton University Press, 2016.
8. Thomas Piketty. *Capital in the Twenty-First Century*. Cambridge, MA: Harvard University Press, 2014; John Bellamy Foster and Robert McChesney. *The Endless Crisis*. New York, NY: Monthly Review Press, 2012; James Galbraith. *The End of Normal*. New York, NY: Simon & Schuster, 2014.
9. Wolfgang Streeck. *How Will Capitalism End? Essays on a Failing System*. New York, NY: Verso, 2017.
10. Ibid., 60.
11. Ibid., 58.
12. Jeremy Rifkin. *The Zero Marginal Cost Society: The Internet of Things, the Collaborative Commons, and the Eclipse of Capitalism*. New York, NY: St. Martin's Press, 2014.
13. Paul Mason. *Postcapitalism: A Guide to Our Future*. New York, NY: Penguin, 2015.
14. Ibid., 27.
15. Ibid., xix.
16. Nick Srnicek and Alex Williams. "Manifesto for an Accelerationist Politics." *Critical Legal Thinking*, May 14, 2013. Retrieved from http://criticallegalthinking.com/2013/05/14/accelerate-manifesto-for-an-accelerationist-politics/; For analysis and critique acceleration in relation to education see Sam Sellar and David R. Cole. "Accelerationism: A Timely Provocation for the Critical Sociology of Education." *British Journal of Sociology of Education* 38, no. 1 (2017): 38–48; Alexander J. Means. "On Accelerationism: Decolonizing Technoscience through Critical Pedagogy." *Journal for Activist Science and Technology Education* 6, no. 1 (2015): 20–27.
17. Srnicek and Williams, 2013.
18. Ibid.
19. J.K. Gibson-Graham. *A Postcapitalist Politics*. Minneapolis: University of Minnesota

Press, 2006; Michael Hardt and Antonio Negri. *Commonwealth*. Cambridge, MA: Harvard, 2009.
20 Walter Mignolo. *The Darker Side of Western Modernity: Global Futures, Decolonial Options*. Durham, NC: Duke, 2011; Chandra Talpade Mohanty. *Feminism Without Borders: Decolonizing Theory, Practicing Solidarity*. Durham, NC: Duke University Press, 2003; Vandana Shiva. *Earth Democracy: Justice, Sustainability and Peace*. London, UK: Zed Books, 2016.
21 Maarten Simons and Jan Masschelein. "The Governmentalization of Learning and the Assemblage of a Learning Apparatus." *Educational Theory* 58, no. 4 (2008): 391–415.
22 Douglas Rushkoff. *Throwing Rocks at the Google Bus*. New York, NY: Penguin, 2016, 4.
23 Richard Wilkinson and Kate Pickett. *The Spirit Level*. New York, NY: Penguin, 2009.
24 See Tim Jackson for a thoughtful rendering of an economics beyond the logic of GDP. *Prosperity Without Growth: Economics for a Finite Planet*. New York, NY: Routledge, 2009.
25 Goran Therborn. *The Killing Fields of Inequality*. Malden, MA: Polity, 2011, 1.
26 *New York* magazine. "The Money–Empathy Gap." Retrieved from http://nymag.com/news/features/money-brain-2012-7/index4.html
27 Jonathan Pearlman. "1 in 5 CEOs Are Psychopaths, Study Finds." *The Telegraph*, September 13, 2016. Retrieved from www.telegraph.co.uk/news/2016/09/13/1-in-5-ceos-are-psychopaths-australian-study-finds/
28 Christian Felber. *Change Everything: Creating an Economy for the Common Good*. London: Zed Books, 2015, 1.
29 Jacques Rancière. *The Politics of Aesthetics*. New York, NY: Bloomsbury, 2013.
30 Noah De Lissovoy. *Education and Emancipation in the Neoliberal Era: Being, Teaching, and Power*. New York, NY: Palgrave, 2015.
31 I have been influenced heavily by the radical democratic tradition. See, for instance, Eric Olin Wright. *Envisioning Real Utopias*. New York, NY: Verso, 2010. Here Wright provides a succinct sociological articulation of radical democratic principles and a sociological theory of social change with a vision of economic democratization as central to both an emancipatory social science as well as social order.
32 An exception is the concept of "study" developed by the educational philosopher Tyson Lewis in his 2013 book on Giorgio Agamben and other publications. My concept of mass intellectuality is somewhat similar to study in the sense that it recognizes the limits of contemporary learning discourses and the need for an alternative value system for learning. However, whereas Lewis juxtaposes the radical non-determination and im-potential of study against the prescriptive determination of learning, mass intellectuality retains a sense of educational direction and orientation. Study as im-potential conceives of learning as *pure freedom* in knowledge construction, including a romantic, anti-productivist ideal of freedom not to learn, not to know, not to engage, not to produce, and not to develop. Lewis' work is brilliant in its articulation. However, this idea of learning as pure freedom, or im-potential, is problematic. Our reality is too serious not to orient learning to specific socially mediated goals and aims. We require a new approach to conceptualizing creativity, imagination, experimentation, and freedom in knowledge construction, but not without direct engagement with problems along with a commitment to developing human capability, which also means developing patterns of intentionality and scientific rigor necessary for moving history forward not only to alleviate suffering and avoid catastrophe but to create new models and patterns of global democratic life.
33 Henry Farrell. "The Thousand Day Reich: The Double Movement." *Crooked Timber*, May 1, 2017. Retrieved from http://crookedtimber.org/2017/05/01/the-thousand-day-reich-the-double-movement/

INDEX

Locators in *italics* refer to figures.

adaptive learning models *101*, 101–102
Agamben, Giorgio 153
age *see* generational precarity
agency: algorithmic education 121; futurity 154
algorithmic education 98–105, *101*, 114–120
algorithmic imaginary 105–106, 108
Alter, Adam 119
analytic grammar 73–76
antagonism, digitization in education 109–113
anti-social attitudes 163–164
Apple 138
arts, university education 90–91
Ashton, David 140
automation 14, 126–128; cognitive capitalism 73–74; creative destruction 128–131; creativity in education 76–78; educational ruptures 139–144; jobless future 131–139; post-work education 144–150
Autor, David 45–46

Baker, Dean 49–50
Ball, Stephen J. 22
Beck, Ulrich 153
beyond the control society 120–122
big data 112

biometric sensors 115–116
Boltanski, Luc 8
Bourdieu, Pierre 26–27
Brown, Phillip 140
Brown, Wendy 32–33, 90–91
Brynjolfsson, Erik 133, 137

capital *see* human capital
capitalism: cognitive 72–77, 87, 91–92; creativity in education 69–70; digitization in education 114–115; education 6–7, 8; futures of 155–160; generational precarity 56–64; solutionism 9–10
capitalist realism 11
Carnevale, Anthony 42–43
Casarino, Cesare 74–75
Case, Anne 147–148
child development, digitization 116–120
China, education 53
Cisco Systems 2–4, 5
cognitive capitalism 72–77, 87, 91–92; *see also* creativity in education
Cold War 80
Collaborative Commons 110–111
Collins, Randall 140–142, 146
commons (majority): creativity in education 78–86; digitization in education 109–113, 121–122; equality 163–166; for

the majority 91–93; sharing economy 76; terminology 74–75
computerization *see* automation; digitization in education
constructivism 28
consumer debt 54–55
corporate managerialism 82–83
Cowen, Tyler 46–49, 145–146, 156
creative destruction, automation 128–131
creative economy 69–73
Creative Industries Taskforce 71
creativity in education 13, 68–69; analytic grammar 73–76; and conflict 76–91; creative economy 69–73; for the majority 91–93
credit 54–55
cynical rationality 11

Darling-Hammond, Linda 118
De Lissovoy, Noah 165
Deaton, Angus 147–148
debt 54–55
Deleuze, Gilles 120
democracy 33, 165–166; *see also* commons (majority)
demographics *see* generational precarity
DeVos, Betsy 9–10, 84–85
digital Taylorism 99–100
digitization in education 13–14, 97–98; algorithmic education 98–105, 114–120; beyond the control society 120–122; neoliberal conflict machine 114–120; optimizing futures 105–113
Dorn, David 45–46
dystopia: automation 138–139; generational precarity 47–48; inequality 10–11

economic growth 161–164
economism in education 12, 17–19; capital 25–28; governance 28–31; human capital 19–23; methodology 23–25; power 31–33
education: automation 139–144, 146–147; as capture 160–166; futurity 154–155; generational precarity 41–43; human capital 19–23; mass intellectuality 166–168; post-work 144–150; problem posing 12; solutionism 2–8; *see also* creativity in education; digitization in education; economism in education

educational change 6
educational purpose 5
educational structure 5–6, 21
educational value 5
EduFactory 76–91
efficiency, digitization in education 99–100
emancipation 164–165
employment: automation 126–128, 131–139, 141–144; capitalism 61–64; digitization in education 107; generational precarity 39–42, 49–56; learning for 42–43, 118, 154–155; post-work 131–139, 144–150; production flows 25–26; solutionism 2–4; STEM jobs 45, 47–48, 52–53, 88; *see also* human capital
ethic of the self 30–31
Ewald, Francis 31–32

false generosity 6
Farrell, Henry 167
Felber, Christian 163–164
Ferreira, Jose 102
financial recession *see* Great Recession (2008)
Fisher, Mark 11
Florida, Richard 71–72
Ford, Martin 133–134
Foster, Bellamy 61, 157
Foucault, Michael 28
Frase, Peter 127, 138
free-markets 28–29
Freire, Paulo 12, 82–83
Friedman, Milton 23, 29
Friedman, Thomas 78–79
futurity 14, 153–155; capitalism 155–160; mass intellectuality 160–168

Galbraith, James 24, 157
Gates, Bill 72, 99
General Motors 138
generational precarity 13, 37–41; education 41–43; human capital 43–46; new feudalism 46–49; policy 49–56; as symptom of crisis 56–64
Gilead, Tal 25
Gingrich, Newt 100
global challenges: creativity in education 77–78; economism in education 17–19; generational precarity 38–39; neoliberalism 9; solutionism 1–3

globalization 45, 70, 80, 131–132
Goldwin, Claudia 44–45
Google 105–106
Gordon, Robert 136, 156
governance, human capital 28–31
Graeber, David 7–8, 148–149
Great Moderation 18
Great Recession (2008): creativity in education 78–79; economism in education 18; futurity 154–155; generational precarity 38–39, 42
growth, economic 161–164

Habermas, Jürgen 103
Hanushek, Eric 21, 26
Haraway, Donna 104–105
Hardt, Michael 74, 76, 80–81
Harvey, David 60, 70, 75
Hayek, Friedrich von 19, 28–29
higher education *see* university
Hill, Steven 112
Howkins, John 71
human capital: automation 127–128; capital 25–28; economism in education 19–23; generational precarity 43–46; governance 28–31; methodology 23–25; power 31–33
hypermeritocracy 47

imagination, futurity 154
immanent critique 8–9
inBloom 121
India, education 53
inequality: capitalism 56–64; dystopia 10–11; economic growth 162–166; economism in education 17–18; employment 54; generational precarity 38–41; human capital 32–33; precarity 37–38; solutionism 4; university 89; *see also* commons (majority)
information society *see* knowledge economy
intellectuality, futurity 154; *see also* mass intellectuality
Internet of Things 109–111

jobs *see* employment
Jobs, Steve 119
Johnson, Robert 10

Kahn, Richard 104
Kalecki, Michal 31

Katz, Lawrence 44–45
Kellner, Douglas 104
Keynes, John Maynard: automation 130, 146; employment 49, 53–54, 55–56
knowledge economy: automation 132, 140; creativity in education 70–71; digitization in education 97–98
knowledge management 87–88
Knowledge Works 106–109
Krugman, Paul 55

labor *see* employment
Lanchester, John 137–138
language, mass intellectuality 167–168
Lauder, Hugh 140
legitimacy crisis 144–150
Lewis, Tyson 155
liberal arts, university education 90–91
Lingard, Bob 21–22
Locke, John 25–26

machine learning 127; *see also* automation
MacLellan, Matthew 4–5
mainstream economics: automation 130–131, 136, 139; human capital 19–20
majority *see* commons (majority); democracy
managerialism 82–83
Marcuse, Herbert 103
market fundamentalism: automation 130, 148; economism in education 23–25; futurity 161–162, 164–166; neoliberalism 6–7
Marxism: automation 129–130, 138; capitalism 59–60, 62, 156; human capital 25–26
Mason, Paul 158–159
mass intellectuality 166–168
Masschelein, Jan 160–161
McAfee, Andrew 133, 137
McChesney, Robert 61, 157
McRae, Phil 118
meritocracy: generational precarity 47–49; human capital 27–28
methodological individualism 24
middle class jobs, automation 134–137, 141–143
Mill, J. S. 128
millennials *see* generational precarity
Mirowski, Philip 30
Moore's Law 133, 136

morality, human capital 30–31
Morozov, Evgeny 2, 112
Murray, Charles 48

National Employment Law Project 50–52
Negri, Antonio 74, 76
neoclassical perspectives: automation 130–131, 139; human capital 19–20, 23–24, 26
neoliberal conflict machine 114–120
neoliberalism: automation 140; creativity in education 80–86, 90–93; democracy 33; education 6–7; global challenges 9; human capital 19–20, 26, 28–29, 31; market fundamentalism 6–7; political context 9
new feudalism 46–49
new prudentialism 28
Newfield, Christopher 76–77

online learning *see* digitization in education
Organisation for Economic Co-operation and Development (OECD) 17–18
overeducation 43

Pasquinelli, Matteo 72
Piketty, Thomas: automation 137; capitalism 56–58; economism in education 24; futurity 155, 156–157
Polanyi, Karl 24–25
policy: creativity in education 80–83; economism in education 25; generational precarity 49–56; Organisation for Economic Co-operation and Development 17–18
political context: automation 138–139; creativity in education 89–93; democracy 33, 165–166; futurity 159–160, 167–168; generational precarity 63–64; human capital 31–33; mass intellectuality 167–168; neoliberalism 9
Post-Keynesianism: automation 146, 147; human capital 19
post-social universities 90–91
post-work education 144–150
post-work future 131–139
power: creativity in education 87–89, 92–93; digitization in education 120–122; human capital 31–33
precarity 37–38; *see also* generational precarity

Pressey, Sidney 98–99
privatization: digitization in education 117–118, 122; inequality 83–84
problem posing 12
production flows 25–26
professional jobs, automation 134–137, 141–143
progressivism: capitalism 146, 158, 159–160; contemporary context 9; creativity in education 80, 82, 85; digitization in education 104, 108, 122; generational precarity 55, 63; mass intellectuality 167–168
psychology: digitization in education 116–117; inequality 163–164; racial context 148

racial context, employment 147–148
Rajan, Raghuram 43–44
Rancière, Jacques 164–165
rationality: cynical 11; neoliberalism 6–7; *see also* market fundamentalism
recession *see* Great Recession (2008)
Reeves, Richard 144
reflexive modernization 153
Ricardo, David 128–129
Rifkin, Jeremy 109–111, 158
Rizvi, Fazal 21–22
robots *see* automation
Romer, Paul 20
Roosevelt, Franklin D., President of USA 37
Rose, Stephen 42–43
Rushkoff, Douglas 162

Say's Law: automation 128–129; employment 49; human capital 44
schools: algorithmic education 98–105; creativity in education 78–86; digitization in education 117–120
Schumpeter, Joseph 24, 129–130
self, human capital 30–31
sharing economy 76; *see also* commons (majority)
Silicon Valley: digitization in education 99, 114, 119–120; dystopia 10; futurity 154; technological progress 2
Silva, Jennifer 40–41
Simons, Maarten 161
skill-biased technological change (SBTC) 44–46, 50

Smith, Adam 23
sociality, futurity 154
society of control 120–122
sociotechnical imaginaries 105–106, 108
solutionism 2–12
Srnicek, Nick 159–160
stagnation, capitalism 56–57, 61–62, 156–158
state, human capital 29–30
STEM employment 45, 47–48, 52–53, 88
Stewart, Thomas 76–77
Stiglitz, Joseph 54
strategic forecasting 106–109
Streeck, Wolfgang: capitalism 62–63, 157–158; cynical rationality 11; economism in education 18–19
subjectification 49

Taylorism 99–100
technological progress: generational precarity 43–48, 49–51; sharing economy 76; solutionism 1–12; *see also* automation; digitization in education
test-based accountability 82–84

Therborn, Goran 163
time horizon 33
transcendence: capitalism 158; digitization in education 109–113
Trump, Donald, President of USA 9

undereducation 42–43
university: creativity in education 86–91; employment advantage 43, 140–141, 143; generational precarity 42–43, 45–46, 51

value, conceptions of 7–8
value structure 4
Varoufakis, Yanis 156
Vercellone, Carlo 73–74, 75

Weber, Max: digitization in education 103; human capital 26
Weeks, Kathi 148
Williams, Alex 159–160
Williamson, Ben 105–106
work *see* employment
Wöβmann, Ludger 21
Wright, Eric Olin 143–144

Zuckerberg, Mark 99